HEART HEALTHY COOKBOOK FOR BEGINNERS

150 Recipes to Delight with Easy & Flavorful Low-Sodium, Low-Fat Creations for Blood Pressure Maintenance and Joyful Living.

Magda Jones

Magda Jones

1st edition

Codice ISBN: 9798866521500

Table of Contents

DOWNLOAD YOUR BONUS NOW!

Exclusive Bonus Content:

Calm Heart, Strong Heart: Embracing Yoga, Meditation, and Deep Breathing"

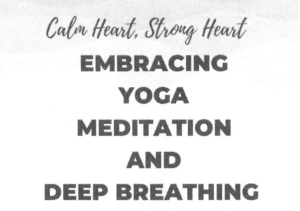

Chapter 1: Understanding Heart Health

The Importance of a Heart-Healthy Diet

In today's fast-paced world, it can be easy to overlook the significance of maintaining a healthy heart. However, cardiovascular diseases continue to be one of the leading causes of death worldwide. The good news is that adopting a heart-healthy diet can significantly reduce the risk of developing these conditions. In this subchapter, we will explore the importance of a heart-healthy diet and how it can benefit you as a beginner in your journey towards optimal heart health.

A heart-healthy diet is not just about cutting out fats and calories; it is about making smart food choices that nourish and support your heart. By incorporating low-fat, nutritious recipes into your daily meals, you can improve your cardiovascular health and overall well-being.

One of the primary benefits of a heart-healthy diet is the reduction in cholesterol levels. High cholesterol is a major risk factor for heart disease and can lead to the formation of arterial plaque, restricting blood flow to the heart. By focusing on low-fat recipes, you can lower your cholesterol levels and promote a healthy blood flow, reducing the risk of heart-related issues.

Furthermore, a heart-healthy diet can help regulate blood pressure. High blood pressure puts strain on the heart and can lead to serious complications. By increasing your intake of fruits, vegetables, whole grains, and lean proteins while minimizing sodium and processed foods, you can maintain healthy blood pressure levels and support a strong heart.

In addition to preventing heart disease, a heart-healthy diet can also aid in weight management. Obesity is closely linked to heart problems, as the excess weight puts stress on your heart and increases the likelihood of developing conditions such as diabetes and hypertension. By following a low-fat, balanced meal plan, you can achieve and maintain a healthy weight, reducing the strain on your heart and improving your overall quality of life.

In conclusion, a heart-healthy diet is essential for beginners looking to support a strong heart and achieve optimal health. By incorporating nutritious, low-fat recipes into your meals and following a 30-day meal plan, you can reduce the risk of heart disease, regulate blood pressure, and manage your weight effectively. This book, "The Heart-Healthy Cookbook for Beginners," is designed to provide you with the expert guidance and delicious recipes you need to embark on a heart-healthy journey. Discover the joy of nourishing your body while promoting a strong heart and optimal well-being.

How Diet Affects Heart Health

A healthy heart is essential for overall well-being, and one of the key factors that influence heart health is our diet. The food we eat plays a crucial role in maintaining a strong and healthy heart. In this subchapter, we will explore how diet affects heart health and provide you with valuable information on making heart-healthy choices.

The Heart-Healthy Cookbook for Beginners is your ultimate guide to nourishing your heart and supporting optimal health. Packed with 150 mouthwatering recipes, this cookbook is specifically designed for beginners who are looking to embark on a heart-healthy journey.

So, how exactly does diet affect heart health? Well, a diet high in saturated and trans fats, cholesterol, and sodium can significantly increase the risk of heart disease. On the other hand, a diet rich in fruits, vegetables, whole grains, lean proteins, and healthy fats can help protect against heart disease.

This cookbook emphasizes the importance of low-fat recipes that not only taste delicious but also support a strong heart. By reducing the amount of saturated and trans fats in your diet, you can lower your cholesterol levels and reduce the risk of plaque buildup in your arteries. The 30-day meal plan included in this book will help you get started on a heart-healthy diet and establish healthy eating habits.

Expert guidance is provided throughout the book to help you make informed choices about your diet. You will learn about the different types of fats and how they impact your heart health. Additionally, you will discover tips and tricks for shopping, meal prepping, and cooking heart-healthy meals that are both nutritious and flavorful.

Whether you are a beginner in the kitchen or a seasoned chef, this cookbook offers a variety of recipes that cater to different tastes and dietary preferences. From breakfast options like whole grain pancakes with fresh berries to satisfying dinners like grilled salmon with quinoa and roasted vegetables, you will find a wide array of options to suit your palate.

Invest in The Heart-Healthy Cookbook for Beginners and embark on a journey towards a healthier heart. Discover the power of nutrition and take control of your heart health today!

Key Nutrients for a Strong Heart

In this subchapter, we will explore the essential nutrients that play a vital role in maintaining a strong and healthy heart. Understanding the significance of these key nutrients will empower you to make informed choices when it comes to your diet and overall heart health.

1. Omega-3 Fatty Acids: Omega-3 fatty acids are known for their ability to reduce inflammation and promote heart health. They can be found in fatty fish such as salmon, mackerel, and sardines. Including these fish in your diet regularly can help lower the risk of heart disease and improve overall cardiovascular health.

2. Fiber: A diet rich in fiber is essential for maintaining a healthy heart. Soluble fiber, found in foods like oats, legumes, and fruits, helps lower cholesterol levels and regulate blood sugar levels. Insoluble fiber, found in whole grains and vegetables, aids in maintaining a healthy weight and preventing conditions like hypertension and heart disease.

3. Antioxidants: Antioxidants are powerful compounds that protect the heart from oxidative stress and inflammation. They can be found in colorful fruits and vegetables, such as berries, leafy greens, and citrus fruits. Including a variety of these antioxidant-rich foods in your diet can help reduce the risk of heart disease and improve overall heart health.

4. Potassium: Potassium is a mineral that plays a crucial role in maintaining a healthy heart rhythm and blood pressure. Including potassium-rich foods such as bananas, avocados, and leafy greens can help regulate blood pressure and reduce the risk of cardiovascular diseases.

5. Magnesium: Magnesium is another essential mineral for heart health. It helps relax blood vessels, regulate blood pressure, and support overall heart function. Foods rich in magnesium include nuts, seeds, whole grains, and leafy greens.

By incorporating these key nutrients into your diet, you can support a strong and healthy heart. The Heart-Healthy Cookbook for Beginners offers a wide range of recipes that are not only delicious but also packed with these essential nutrients. With a 30-day meal plan and expert guidance, this cookbook provides everything you need to embark on a heart-healthy journey.

Discover 150 delicious and nutritious low-fat recipes that will not only satisfy your taste buds but also support your heart health. Whether you are a beginner or an experienced cook, this cookbook is tailored to meet the needs of those who prioritize heart health. With expert guidance and a focus on optimal health, you can enjoy the journey towards a stronger heart and a healthier life.

The Role of Fats in Heart Health

When it comes to maintaining a healthy heart, understanding the role of fats is crucial. Contrary to popular belief, not all fats are bad for you. In fact, certain types of fats are essential for optimal heart health. In this subchapter, we will delve into the different types of fats and their impact on your heart.

Firstly, it is important to distinguish between healthy fats and unhealthy fats. Saturated and trans fats are the ones to avoid as they can raise your cholesterol levels and increase the risk of heart disease. These fats are commonly found in processed foods, fried foods, and fatty cuts of meat.

On the other hand, unsaturated fats, particularly monounsaturated and polyunsaturated fats, are the good fats that support a strong heart. These fats can help lower cholesterol levels and reduce the risk of heart disease. They are found in foods such as avocados, nuts, seeds, and fatty fish like salmon and mackerel.

Omega-3 fatty acids, a type of polyunsaturated fat, are especially beneficial for heart health. They have been shown to decrease inflammation, lower triglyceride levels, and improve overall heart function. Including foods rich in omega-3s, like flaxseeds, chia seeds, and walnuts, in your diet can have a positive impact on your heart.

It is important to note that while fats are essential, they should still be consumed in moderation. Even healthy fats contain calories, so it is important to maintain a balanced diet and watch your portion sizes. In our heart-healthy cookbook, you will find 150 delicious low-fat recipes that are not only nutritious but also support your heart health.

Our cookbook is specifically designed for beginners in the world of heart-healthy cooking. It includes a 30-day meal plan to help you kickstart your journey towards a stronger heart. Our recipes are crafted by experts in the field, ensuring that you receive the best guidance for optimal health.

Discover the joy of cooking and eating delicious meals that nourish your heart. With our cookbook as your guide, you can improve your heart health without sacrificing flavor. Say goodbye to unhealthy fats and hello to a stronger, healthier heart. Start your journey towards a heart-healthy lifestyle today!

Reading Food Labels for Heart Health

When it comes to maintaining a healthy heart, understanding how to read food labels is crucial. The food we consume plays a significant role in our overall well-being, especially when it comes to heart health. In this subchapter, we will guide you through the process of reading food labels, allowing you to make informed choices and support your strong heart.

Food labels provide essential information about the nutritional content of a product. By examining these labels, you can identify potential risks and make healthier choices. Here are some key points to consider:

1. Serving Size: Pay attention to the serving size listed on the label. This information will help you determine the amount of nutrients you are consuming.

2. Total Fat: Look for products that are low in saturated and trans fats. These fats can raise your cholesterol levels and increase the risk of heart disease. Opt for foods with healthier fats, such as monounsaturated and polyunsaturated fats.

3. Sodium: Excessive sodium intake can lead to high blood pressure, which is a major risk factor for heart disease. Choose products with lower sodium content and limit your overall sodium intake.

4. Cholesterol: Keep an eye on the cholesterol content in food labels. High cholesterol levels can contribute to the development of heart disease. Aim for products with low or no cholesterol.

5. Fiber: Fiber is essential for a healthy heart. Look for foods high in dietary fiber, as it can help reduce cholesterol levels and promote heart health.

6. Added Sugars: Sugar consumption has been linked to various cardiovascular issues. Be mindful of the amount of added sugars in the products you choose. Opt for foods with little to no added sugars.

By understanding and utilizing the information provided on food labels, you can make conscious decisions to support your heart health. Incorporating heart-healthy recipes into your diet is another crucial step towards optimal well-being.

"The Heart-Healthy Cookbook for Beginners" offers a wide range of nutritious and mouthwatering dishes designed specifically for heart health. With a 30-day meal plan and expert guidance, this cookbook is the ultimate resource for those looking to embark on a heart-healthy culinary journey.

Discover the joy of preparing and savoring delicious low-fat meals that will nourish your body and support your strong heart. With the help of this cookbook, you can take control of your diet and enjoy the benefits of a heart-healthy lifestyle.

Remember, your heart health is in your hands, and by reading food labels and choosing the right ingredients, you can pave the way for a healthier future.

Chapter 2: Getting Started with a Heart-Healthy Lifestyle

Assessing Your Current Diet and Habits

Before embarking on a journey towards a healthier heart, it is essential to assess your current diet and habits. Understanding where you stand will help you make necessary changes and set realistic goals. In this subchapter, we will guide you through the process of evaluating your eating patterns and lifestyle choices, enabling you to make informed decisions for optimal heart health.

Start by keeping a food diary for at least a week. This simple yet powerful tool will provide you with a clear picture of what you consume on a daily basis. Note down everything you eat and drink, including portion sizes, preparation methods, and any snacks or beverages consumed between meals. Be honest with yourself and record every detail. This will help identify areas where improvements can be made.

Once you have a comprehensive record of your diet, analyze it critically. Look for patterns or trends that may be impacting your heart health. Are you consuming excessive amounts of saturated fats, cholesterol, or sodium? Do you rely heavily on processed or fast food? Are fruits, vegetables, and whole grains lacking in your meals? Identifying these potential pitfalls will enable you to address them effectively.

Apart from your diet, it is crucial to evaluate your lifestyle habits. Assess your physical activity level, stress levels, and sleep patterns. Regular exercise is vital for a healthy heart, so consider how often and how intensely you engage in physical activity. Evaluate your stress management techniques, as chronic stress can have detrimental effects on your cardiovascular system. Additionally, examine your sleep habits and strive to ensure you are getting adequate rest.

Understanding your current diet and habits will serve as a foundation for creating a personalized heart-healthy plan. With the guidance of "The Heart-Healthy Cookbook for Beginners," you will have access to a wealth of nutritious and delicious recipes. These recipes, combined with the expert guidance provided, will support your journey towards optimal heart health.

In the upcoming chapters, we will delve deeper into the 30-day meal plan designed to incorporate these delicious low-fat recipes. We will also provide additional expert advice on how to make sustainable changes to your diet and lifestyle. By following this comprehensive approach, you will not only improve your heart health but also enhance your overall well-being. Embark on this journey today and discover the joy of nourishing your heart with delicious and nutritious meals.

Setting Realistic Goals for Heart Health

Introduction:In order to maintain a healthy heart, it is essential to set realistic goals and make the necessary lifestyle changes. This subchapter will guide you on how to set achievable goals for improving heart health, ensuring that you can enjoy a long and fulfilling life. By making small, gradual changes, you can create a sustainable plan to support your heart health journey.

Understanding Your Current Status:Before setting goals, it is crucial to assess your current heart health. This includes evaluating your diet, physical activity level, and overall lifestyle. By understanding where you stand, you can determine the areas that require improvement and set realistic targets accordingly.

Goal-Setting Guidelines:1. Start Small: Begin by setting small, attainable goals that are specific, measurable, and time-bound. For example, aim to incorporate one heart-healthy recipe into your weekly meal plan or commit to walking for 30 minutes three times a week.2. Gradual Progression: As you become comfortable with your initial goals, gradually increase the intensity or duration of your activities. This ensures that you continue challenging yourself without becoming overwhelmed.3. Seek Expert Guidance: Consult with a healthcare professional or nutritionist who specializes in heart health. They can provide personalized guidance and help you set realistic goals based on your unique circumstances.4. Monitor Progress: Regularly assess your progress to stay motivated and make adjustments if needed. Tracking your achievements will help you stay on track and celebrate milestones along the way.

Creating a Supportive Environment:To achieve your heart health goals, it is essential to create an environment that supports your efforts. Surround yourself with like-minded individuals who share similar health goals. Engage in activities that promote heart health, such as joining a walking club or participating in cooking classes that focus on heart-healthy recipes.

Conclusion:By setting realistic goals for heart health, you can make significant strides in improving your overall well-being. Remember to start small, seek professional guidance, and monitor your progress along the way. With dedication and perseverance, you can achieve optimal heart health and enjoy the benefits of a strong and resilient heart.

Creating a Heart-Healthy Meal Plan

Maintaining a strong and healthy heart is essential for overall well-being, and one of the most effective ways to support heart health is through a well-balanced and nutritious meal plan. In this subchapter, we will explore the key principles of creating a heart-healthy meal plan, providing you with expert guidance and 150 delicious low-fat recipes to support your journey towards optimal heart health.

When it comes to heart-healthy eating, it is crucial to focus on nutrient-dense foods that promote cardiovascular wellness. This means incorporating a variety of fruits, vegetables, whole grains, lean proteins, and healthy fats into your diet. Our cookbook is specifically designed for beginners in the realm of heart-healthy cooking, making it easy for you to discover and prepare delicious meals that are beneficial for your heart.

To assist you further, we have also included a 30-day meal plan to help you get started on your heart-healthy journey. This plan takes away the guesswork and provides you with a comprehensive guide on what to eat for breakfast, lunch, dinner, and snacks. By following this plan, you can ensure that you are getting a wide range of nutrients while keeping your fat intake in check.

Our recipes are carefully crafted to be low in fat, but without compromising on flavor. From hearty soups and salads to satisfying main courses and delectable desserts, our cookbook covers it all. You can explore a variety of cuisines and flavors while keeping your heart health in mind.

In addition to the delicious recipes, our book provides expert guidance on how to optimize your heart health. You will find valuable information on portion control, cooking techniques, and tips for making heart-healthy choices when dining out. By arming yourself with knowledge, you can make informed decisions that positively impact your heart health.

Discover 150 Delicious and Nutritious Low-Fat Recipes to Support a Strong Heart. Includes a 30-Day Meal Plan, and Expert Guidance for Optimal Health! Dive into the world of heart-healthy cooking with our comprehensive cookbook designed for beginners. Say goodbye to bland meals and hello to flavorful dishes that support your heart health. With our guidance and delicious recipes, you can embark on a journey towards a stronger and healthier heart.

Stocking Your Pantry with Heart-Healthy Ingredients

In order to support a strong and healthy heart, it is essential to stock your pantry with the right ingredients. By filling your kitchen with heart-healthy foods, you can ensure that you are always prepared to create delicious and nutritious low-fat meals. This subchapter will guide you through the essential ingredients you need to have on hand, making it easier for you to follow the 150 delicious low-fat recipes in "The Heart-Healthy Cookbook for Beginners."

First and foremost, whole grains are the foundation of a heart-healthy pantry. They are rich in fiber, vitamins, and minerals that promote cardiovascular health. Stock up on brown rice, quinoa, whole wheat pasta, and oats. These versatile ingredients can be used in a variety of dishes, from hearty salads to comforting porridge.

Next, include an array of fruits and vegetables in your pantry. These colorful and nutrient-packed foods are low in calories and high in antioxidants, which can help reduce the risk of heart disease. Opt for fresh produce when available, but also keep frozen fruits and vegetables on hand for when fresh options are not readily available.

Lean proteins are another crucial component of a heart-healthy pantry. Choose lean cuts of poultry, such as skinless chicken breasts or turkey, as well as fish like salmon or trout, which are rich in omega-3 fatty acids. Plant-based protein sources like beans, lentils, and tofu are also excellent options.

Healthy fats play a crucial role in maintaining heart health. Stock up on sources of monounsaturated fats, such as olive oil, avocado, and nuts like almonds and walnuts. These fats can help lower bad cholesterol levels and reduce the risk of heart disease.

Lastly, don't forget about herbs, spices, and condiments. These ingredients can add flavor to your dishes without adding excess salt or unhealthy fats. Experiment with herbs like basil, thyme, and rosemary, and spices such as turmeric, cinnamon, and cayenne pepper. Also, keep a variety of vinegars, low-sodium soy sauce, and mustards in your pantry to enhance the taste of your meals.

By stocking your pantry with these heart-healthy ingredients, you will always have the necessary building blocks to create nutritious and delicious meals. With "The Heart-Healthy Cookbook for Beginners" as your guide, and armed with a well-stocked pantry, you can embark on a journey towards optimal heart health and overall well-being.

Tips for Heart-Healthy Grocery Shopping

Maintaining a heart-healthy diet is crucial for supporting a strong heart and overall optimal health. When it comes to grocery shopping, making the right choices can significantly impact your heart health. Here are some essential tips to keep in mind while navigating the aisles and selecting the best ingredients for your heart-healthy meals.

1. Plan Ahead: Before heading to the grocery store, take some time to plan your meals for the week. This will help you create a shopping list and ensure you have all the necessary ingredients on hand. Planning ahead can also help you avoid impulse purchases of unhealthy foods.

2. Read Labels: When selecting packaged foods, always read the nutrition labels. Look for foods that are low in saturated and trans fats, cholesterol, and sodium. Opt for products that are high in fiber, whole grains, and unsaturated fats like omega-3 fatty acids.

3. Choose Fresh Produce: Fill your cart with a variety of fresh fruits and vegetables. These nutrient-rich foods are low in calories and packed with vitamins, minerals, and antioxidants that are beneficial for heart health. Aim for a colorful assortment to ensure you're getting a wide range of nutrients.

4. Go for Lean Proteins: Choose lean sources of protein, such as skinless poultry, fish, legumes, and tofu. These options are low in saturated fat and cholesterol, making them heart-healthy choices. Limit your consumption of red meat and opt for lean cuts when you do indulge.

5. Incorporate Whole Grains: Swap refined grains for whole grains like whole wheat, quinoa, brown rice, and oats. These grains are higher in fiber and other essential nutrients, which can help lower cholesterol levels and reduce the risk of heart disease.

6. Limit Added Sugars: Be cautious of foods and beverages that contain added sugars, such as sugary drinks, candies, and processed snacks. Excessive sugar consumption has been linked to an increased risk of heart disease. Instead, satisfy your sweet tooth with naturally sweetened options like fresh fruits.

7. Shop the Perimeter: The outer aisles of the grocery store are typically where the freshest and healthiest foods reside. Focus on filling your cart with items from these areas, such as fresh produce, lean proteins, and dairy products. Limit your time in the processed food sections in the center aisles.

By following these tips, you can make heart-healthy choices during your grocery shopping trips. Remember, a well-balanced diet and regular exercise are key components of maintaining a healthy heart. With the right ingredients and recipes, you can embark on a delicious journey to support your heart health and overall well-being.

Chapter 3: Expert Guidance for Optimal Heart Health

<u>Understanding Cholesterol and Blood Pressure</u>

Maintaining a healthy heart requires a comprehensive understanding of the factors that can impact its well-being. Two major contributors to heart disease are high cholesterol levels and high blood pressure. In this subchapter, we will delve into the intricacies of cholesterol and blood pressure, helping you gain insight into how these factors affect your heart health.

Cholesterol, often referred to as the "silent killer," is a waxy substance found in the blood. While our bodies need cholesterol to build healthy cells, high levels of LDL (low-density lipoprotein) cholesterol can lead to plaque buildup in the arteries, increasing the risk of heart disease. On the other hand, HDL (high-density lipoprotein) cholesterol is considered the "good" cholesterol as it helps remove LDL cholesterol from the bloodstream.

To combat high cholesterol levels, a heart-healthy diet is essential. The Heart-Healthy Cookbook offers 150 delicious low-fat recipes specially designed for beginners. These recipes not only taste great but also promote low cholesterol levels, reducing the risk of heart disease. From flavorful salads to hearty soups and satisfying main courses, you will find a variety of options to suit your taste buds and support your strong heart.

Another crucial aspect of heart health is blood pressure. Blood pressure refers to the force exerted by blood against the walls of the arteries. High blood pressure, or hypertension, can damage the arteries over time, leading to heart disease, stroke, and other serious health issues. A balanced diet, regular exercise, and managing stress levels are vital in maintaining healthy blood pressure.

Within this subchapter, you will find expert guidance on how to manage your blood pressure through dietary choices. The 30-day meal plan provided in The Heart-Healthy Cookbook will help you structure your meals to support optimal heart health and keep your blood pressure in check. Additionally, you will discover tips and tricks to reduce sodium intake, incorporate nutrient-rich foods, and make heart-healthy choices when dining out.

By understanding the impact of cholesterol and blood pressure on heart health, and armed with delicious low-fat recipes and expert guidance, you will embark on a journey towards a healthier heart. The Heart-Healthy Cookbook is your ultimate resource for discovering 150 delicious and nutritious low-fat recipes, supporting a strong heart, and achieving optimal health. Start your journey today and experience the benefits of a heart-healthy lifestyle!

Incorporating Exercise into Your Heart-Healthy Lifestyle

Maintaining a heart-healthy lifestyle is not just about eating nutritious meals; it also involves incorporating regular exercise into your daily routine. Exercise plays a crucial role in keeping your heart strong and reducing the risk of heart disease. In this subchapter, we will explore the various ways you can include exercise into your heart-healthy lifestyle.

First and foremost, it's important to consult with your healthcare provider before starting any exercise regimen, especially if you have pre-existing heart conditions. Once you have the green light, you can begin slowly and gradually increase the intensity of your workouts.

Aerobic exercises, such as brisk walking, jogging, swimming, or cycling, are excellent choices for improving cardiovascular health. Aim for at least 150 minutes of moderate-intensity aerobic exercise per week, or 75 minutes of vigorous-intensity exercise if you're up for the challenge. You can break these sessions into shorter intervals to make it more manageable.

Strength training is equally important for a strong heart. Incorporate resistance exercises, such as lifting weights or using resistance bands, into your routine two to three times a week. These exercises help build muscular strength and endurance, which can reduce the workload on your heart.

Additionally, don't forget to include flexibility exercises like stretching or yoga to improve your range of motion and prevent injuries. These exercises can also help you relax and reduce stress, which is beneficial for your heart health.

Finding activities you enjoy is key to sticking to an exercise routine. Whether it's dancing, playing a sport, or hiking, make sure to choose activities that make you happy and keep you motivated. Consider joining fitness classes or finding a workout buddy to make exercise more enjoyable and social.

Remember, consistency is key. Aim for at least 30 minutes of exercise most days of the week, but don't be too hard on yourself if you miss a day or two. The important thing is to get back on track and keep moving forward.

Incorporating exercise into your heart-healthy lifestyle will not only benefit your cardiovascular health but also improve your overall well-being. Stay committed, stay active, and enjoy the journey to a stronger heart!

Managing Stress for a Strong Heart

In our fast-paced and demanding world, stress has become an inevitable part of our lives. However, it is crucial to understand that chronic stress can have a detrimental effect on our overall health, particularly our heart. Studies have shown a strong link between chronic stress and heart disease, making stress management an essential component of maintaining a healthy heart. In this subchapter, we will explore some effective strategies for managing stress and supporting a strong heart.

One of the most effective ways to manage stress is through regular exercise. Physical activity releases endorphins, also known as the "feel-good" hormones, which help reduce stress and promote a sense of well-being. Engaging in activities such as brisk walking, swimming, or cycling not only reduces stress levels but also strengthens the heart and improves cardiovascular health.

Another important aspect of stress management is adopting relaxation techniques. Deep breathing exercises, meditation, and yoga have been proven to reduce stress levels and promote a calm state of mind. These practices help activate the body's relaxation response, which counteracts the harmful effects of stress on the heart.

In addition to exercise and relaxation techniques, it is essential to prioritize self-care. Taking time for oneself, engaging in hobbies, spending quality time with loved ones, and practicing mindfulness can all contribute to reducing stress levels. By focusing on self-care, individuals can better manage stress, leading to a healthier heart.

Furthermore, a well-balanced diet plays a crucial role in managing stress and promoting heart health. Consuming nutrient-rich foods, such as fruits, vegetables, whole grains, and lean proteins, provides the body with essential vitamins and minerals that support overall well-being. Additionally, avoiding excessive consumption of caffeine, alcohol, and processed foods can help reduce stress levels and support a strong heart.

Lastly, seeking support from loved ones or professional counselors can be beneficial for managing stress. Talking about feelings and concerns with trusted individuals can provide a sense of relief and help in finding solutions to stressors.

In conclusion, managing stress is vital for maintaining a strong and healthy heart. By incorporating regular exercise, relaxation techniques, self-care practices, a balanced diet, and seeking support, individuals can effectively manage stress levels and support optimal heart health. Remember, a healthy heart starts with managing stress.Maintaining a Healthy Weight for Heart Health

In today's fast-paced world, maintaining a healthy weight is crucial for optimal heart health. Excess weight not only puts a strain on your heart but also increases the risk of developing chronic conditions such as high blood pressure, diabetes, and cardiovascular diseases. However, achieving and maintaining a healthy weight doesn't have to be a daunting task. With the right knowledge and guidance, anyone can embark on a journey towards a stronger heart and overall well-being.

"The Heart-Healthy Cookbook for Beginners" is your ultimate guide to discovering 150 delicious and nutritious low-fat recipes that will support a strong heart. More than just a cookbook, this comprehensive resource provides a 30-day meal plan and expert guidance to help you achieve optimal health.

One of the key components of maintaining a healthy weight for heart health is adopting a balanced diet. This book provides a wide range of low-fat recipes that are not only flavorful but also packed with essential nutrients. From breakfast options like oatmeal with fresh fruits to satisfying main courses like grilled salmon with roasted vegetables, these recipes will keep your taste buds happy while promoting a healthier weight.

Additionally, the "Heart-Healthy Cookbook" emphasizes portion control and mindful eating. By learning to listen to your body's hunger and fullness cues, you can avoid overeating and make healthier choices. The book provides expert guidance on portion sizes and tips for mindful eating, empowering you to take control of your eating habits and maintain a healthy weight.

Regular physical activity is another crucial element in maintaining a healthy weight and promoting heart health. The book includes tips on incorporating exercise into your daily routine and suggests activities that are suitable for beginners. By combining a balanced diet with regular exercise, you can achieve optimal heart health and overall well-being.

Whether you are a beginner in the kitchen or a seasoned cook, "The Heart-Healthy Cookbook for Beginners" is your go-to resource for heart-healthy cooking. With its extensive collection of recipes, 30-day meal plan, and expert guidance, this book will empower you to make healthier choices, maintain a healthy weight, and support a strong heart. Start your journey towards optimal heart health today!

Regular Check-ups and Monitoring for Heart Health

Regular check-ups and monitoring are essential for maintaining a healthy heart. In this subchapter, we will explore the importance of routine check-ups and monitoring for heart health and provide you with expert guidance to support your journey towards optimal heart health.

Regular check-ups with your healthcare provider are crucial for preventing and managing heart diseases. During these check-ups, your doctor will assess your overall health, check your blood pressure, cholesterol levels, and perform various tests to evaluate your heart's function. These routine check-ups allow for early detection of any potential issues and help in managing them before they progress into more severe conditions.

Monitoring your heart health at home is equally important. Regularly measuring your blood pressure and keeping track of your cholesterol levels can provide valuable insights into your heart's well-being. This self-monitoring enables you to make proactive changes to your lifestyle and diet to manage any potential risks.

To support your heart health journey, "The Heart-Healthy Cookbook for Beginners" offers a comprehensive 30-day meal plan designed by experts in the field. This meal plan incorporates 150 delicious and nutritious low-fat recipes specifically tailored to promote a strong heart and overall well-being.

By following the meal plan and incorporating these heart-healthy recipes into your everyday life, you can take charge of your heart health and make positive changes to your diet. The cookbook provides detailed nutritional information for each recipe, ensuring that you have the necessary tools to make informed decisions about your diet and maintain a heart-healthy lifestyle.

Furthermore, the book offers expert guidance on optimal health, including tips on exercise routines, stress management techniques, and lifestyle changes that can significantly improve heart health. By implementing these recommendations, you can enhance your overall well-being and reduce the risk of heart disease.

In conclusion, regular check-ups and monitoring are vital for maintaining a healthy heart. "The Heart-Healthy Cookbook for Beginners" provides you with a comprehensive guide to support your heart health journey. With its 30-day meal plan, expert guidance, and delicious low-fat recipes, you can make positive changes to your diet and lifestyle, ensuring a strong and healthy heart for years to come.

Breakfast Recipes

Wholesome Oat and Berry Parfait

⭐⭐⭐⭐⭐ | Preparation Time: 10 mins | Cooking Time: 0 mins | Portion Size: 2

Ingredients:

- 1 cup rolled oats
- 1.5 cups Greek yogurt (low-fat)
- 1 cup mixed berries (blueberries, raspberries, strawberries)
- 2 tbsp honey
- 1 tbsp chia seeds
- 2 tbsp granola

Instructions:

1. In a glass or jar, start with a layer of rolled oats at the bottom.
2. Add a layer of Greek yogurt on top.
3. Add a generous layer of mixed berries.
4. Drizzle honey over the berries.
5. Repeat the layers until the glass or jar is filled.
6. Sprinkle chia seeds and granola on top.
7. Chill in the refrigerator for 30 minutes before serving.

Nutritional Data: Calories: 280 | Carbohydrates: 45g | Protein: 10g | Fat: 7g | Fiber: 6g

Spinach and Mushroom Egg White Omelette

⭐⭐⭐⭐ | Preparation Time: 10 mins | Cooking Time: 8 mins | Portion Size: 1

Ingredients:

- 3 egg whites
- 1/2 cup spinach (chopped)
- 1/4 cup mushrooms (sliced)
- 1/4 cup feta cheese (crumbled)
- Salt and pepper to taste
- 1 tsp olive oil

Instructions:

1. In a bowl, whisk the egg whites until frothy.
2. Add salt and pepper.
3. Heat olive oil in a non-stick skillet over medium heat.
4. Sauté mushrooms until they release their moisture.
5. Add spinach and cook until wilted.
6. Pour the egg whites over the spinach and mushrooms.
7. Cook until the omelette starts to set around the edges.
8. Sprinkle feta cheese over one half of the omelette.
9. Fold the other half over the cheese.
10. Cook for an additional 2-3 minutes or until fully set.

Nutritional Data: Calories: 150 | Carbohydrates: 3g | Protein: 16g | Fat: 8g | Fiber: 1g

Quinoa and Fruit Breakfast Salad

⭐⭐⭐⭐ | Preparation Time: 10 mins | Cooking Time: 15 mins | Portion Size: 2

Ingredients:

- 1 cup cooked quinoa (cooled)
- 1/2 cup chopped mango

- 1/2 cup strawberries (sliced)
- 1/4 cup blueberries
- 2 tbsp chopped mint leaves
- Juice of 1 lemon
- 1 tbsp honey
- A pinch of salt

Instructions:

1. In a large bowl, mix the cooked quinoa, mango, strawberries, and blueberries.
2. In a separate bowl, whisk together the lemon juice, honey, and salt.
3. Pour the dressing over the quinoa and fruit mixture.
4. Toss to combine.
5. Garnish with chopped mint leaves before serving.

Nutritional Data: Calories: 220 | Carbohydrates: 45g | Protein: 5g | Fat: 2.5g | Fiber: 5g

Heart-Loving Almond Butter Toast with Sliced Strawberries

★★★★★ | Preparation Time: 5 mins | Cooking Time: 2 mins | Portion Size: 1

Ingredients:

- 2 slices of whole-grain bread
- 2 tbsp almond butter
- 5-6 strawberries (sliced)
- 1 tsp chia seeds

Instructions:

1. Toast the slices of whole-grain bread to your desired level of crispness.
2. Spread almond butter generously on each slice.
3. Arrange sliced strawberries on top of the almond butter.
4. Sprinkle chia seeds over the strawberries.

Nutritional Data: Calories: 320 | Carbohydrates: 35g | Protein: 10g | Fat: 17g | Fiber: 9g

Mango and Chia Seed Smoothie Bowl

★★★★★ | Preparation Time: 10 mins | Cooking Time: 0 mins | Portion Size: 1

Ingredients:

- 1 ripe mango (peeled and chopped)
- 1/2 banana
- 1 cup almond milk
- 2 tbsp chia seeds
- 1 tbsp honey
- A handful of granola
- A few blueberries for garnish

Instructions:

1. In a blender, combine the mango, banana, almond milk, and honey.
2. Blend until smooth.
3. Pour the mixture into a bowl.
4. Stir in the chia seeds and allow to sit for a few minutes.
5. Top with granola and blueberries before serving.

Nutritional Data: Calories: 310 | Carbohydrates: 60g | Protein: 7g | Fat: 7g | Fiber: 10g

Sweet Potato and Black Bean Breakfast Burrito

★★★★★ | Preparation Time: 15 mins | Cooking Time: 20 mins | Portion Size: 2

Ingredients:

- 1 large sweet potato (diced)
- 1 cup black beans (cooked or canned, rinsed and drained)
- 2 whole grain tortillas
- 1/2 avocado (sliced)

- 2 tbsp salsa
- 1 tsp olive oil
- Salt and pepper to taste
- 1 tsp ground cumin

Instructions:

1. Heat olive oil in a skillet over medium heat.
2. Add diced sweet potatoes and cook until softened, stirring occasionally.
3. Add the black beans and season with salt, pepper, and cumin. Stir well.
4. Continue to cook for another 5 minutes until everything is heated through.
5. Warm the tortillas as per package instructions.
6. Lay out each tortilla, place a generous scoop of the sweet potato and black bean mixture on each.
7. Top with avocado slices and salsa.
8. Roll up the burrito, tucking in the sides as you go.

Nutritional Data: Calories: 420 | Carbohydrates: 68g | Protein: 12g | Fat: 12g | Fiber: 15g

---

Golden Turmeric and Ginger Porridge

★ ★ ★ ★ ★ | Preparation Time: 5 mins | Cooking Time: 10 mins | Portion Size: 2

Ingredients:

- 1 cup rolled oats
- 2 cups almond milk
- 1 tsp turmeric powder
- 1/2 tsp ground ginger
- 1 tbsp honey
- A pinch of black pepper
- Fresh berries and chopped nuts for garnish

Instructions:

1. In a saucepan, combine rolled oats, almond milk, turmeric, ginger, and black pepper.
2. Cook over medium heat, stirring regularly until the oats are soft and the porridge is creamy.
3. Remove from heat and stir in honey.
4. Serve warm, garnished with fresh berries and chopped nuts.

Nutritional Data: Calories: 270 | Carbohydrates: 45g | Protein: 8g | Fat: 7g | Fiber: 6g

---

Heart-Healthy Blueberry Pancakes (with Almond Flour)

★ ★ ★ ★ ★ | Preparation Time: 10 mins | Cooking Time: 15 mins | Portion Size: 2

Ingredients:

- 1 cup almond flour
- 2 eggs
- 1/4 cup almond milk
- 1/2 cup fresh blueberries
- 1 tsp baking powder
- 1 tsp vanilla extract
- Pinch of salt
- Olive oil or coconut oil for cooking

Instructions:

1. In a mixing bowl, combine almond flour, baking powder, and salt.
2. In a separate bowl, whisk together eggs, almond milk, and vanilla extract.
3. Combine the wet and dry ingredients and fold in the blueberries.
4. Heat a non-stick skillet over medium heat with a small amount of oil.
5. Pour 1/4 cup of batter for each pancake onto the skillet. Cook until bubbles form on the surface, then flip and cook the other side.
6. Serve warm with a drizzle of honey or maple syrup.

Nutritional Data: Calories: 320 | Carbohydrates: 12g | Protein: 12g | Fat: 26g | Fiber: 5g

---

Zesty Lemon and Poppy Seed Overnight Oats

⭐ ⭐ ⭐ ⭐ ⭐ | Preparation Time: 10 mins | Cooking Time: 0 mins (Chill overnight) | Portion Size: 2

Ingredients:
- 1 cup rolled oats
- 1 cup Greek yogurt (low-fat)
- 1/2 cup almond milk
- 1 tbsp poppy seeds
- Zest and juice of 1 lemon
- 2 tbsp honey

Instructions:
1. In a mixing bowl, combine rolled oats, Greek yogurt, almond milk, lemon zest, lemon juice, and honey.
2. Stir well until all ingredients are well combined.
3. Fold in the poppy seeds.
4. Divide the mixture between two jars or containers.
5. Cover and chill in the refrigerator overnight.
6. In the morning, give it a good stir and enjoy cold.

Nutritional Data: Calories: 290 | Carbohydrates: 45g | Protein: 12g | Fat: 7g | Fiber: 6g

---

Nutty Banana and Flaxseed Muffins

⭐ ⭐ ⭐ ⭐ ⭐ | Preparation Time: 15 mins | Cooking Time: 20 mins | Portion Size: 12 muffins **Ingredients:**
- 2 ripe bananas (mashed)
- 1.5 cups whole wheat flour
- 1/2 cup ground flaxseed
- 1/2 cup chopped walnuts
- 2 eggs
- 1/4 cup honey or maple syrup
- 1/2 cup almond milk
- 1 tsp baking powder
- 1 tsp vanilla extract
- Pinch of salt

Instructions:
1. Preheat oven to 375°F (190°C) and line a muffin tin with paper liners.
2. In a mixing bowl, combine the mashed bananas, eggs, honey, almond milk, and vanilla extract.
3. In another bowl, mix the whole wheat flour, ground flaxseed, baking powder, and salt.
4. Gradually incorporate the dry ingredients into the wet mixture.
5. Fold in the chopped walnuts.
6. Spoon the batter into the muffin tin, filling each about two-thirds full.
7. Bake for 20 minutes or until a toothpick inserted into the center comes out clean.
8. Allow to cool before serving.

Nutritional Data: Calories: 170 | Carbohydrates: 25g | Protein: 5g | Fat: 6g | Fiber: 4g

---

Kale, Tofu, and Sun-Dried Tomato Scramble

⭐ ⭐ ⭐ ⭐ ⭐ | Preparation Time: 10 mins | Cooking Time: 12 mins | Portion Size: 2

Ingredients:
- 1 cup firm tofu (crumbled)
- 1 cup kale (chopped)
- 1/4 cup sun-dried tomatoes (chopped)
- 1 tbsp olive oil

- 2 garlic cloves (minced)
- 1 tsp nutritional yeast (optional)
- Salt and pepper to taste

Instructions:

1. Heat olive oil in a skillet over medium heat.
2. Add the minced garlic and sauté until fragrant.
3. Incorporate the crumbled tofu and cook for 5 minutes, stirring occasionally.
4. Add the chopped kale and sun-dried tomatoes, mixing well.
5. Season with salt, pepper, and nutritional yeast if using.
6. Cook until the kale is wilted and the tofu is golden brown.
7. Serve warm with a slice of whole grain toast.

Nutritional Data: Calories: 210 | Carbohydrates: 12g | Protein: 12g | Fat: 14g | Fiber: 3g

Cinnamon Walnut Quinoa Breakfast Pudding

☆ ☆ ☆ ☆ ☆ | Preparation Time: 5 mins | Cooking Time: 15 mins | Portion Size: 2

Ingredients:

- 1 cup cooked quinoa
- 1 cup almond milk
- 1/4 cup walnuts (chopped)
- 2 tbsp honey or maple syrup
- 1 tsp ground cinnamon
- A pinch of salt

Instructions:

1. In a saucepan, combine the cooked quinoa and almond milk. Cook over medium heat.
2. Stir in the cinnamon, honey, and a pinch of salt.

3. Allow the mixture to simmer for 10 minutes until it reaches a pudding-like consistency.
4. Remove from heat and stir in the chopped walnuts.
5. Serve warm, garnished with a sprinkle of cinnamon or fresh berries.

Nutritional Data: Calories: 280 | Carbohydrates: 40g | Protein: 8g | Fat: 10g | Fiber: 4g

Tangy Greek Yogurt with Mixed Berries and Honey Drizzle

☆ ☆ ☆ ☆ ☆ | Preparation Time: 5 mins | Cooking Time: 0 mins | Portion Size: 2

Ingredients:

- 1.5 cups Greek yogurt (low-fat)
- 1 cup mixed berries (blueberries, raspberries, strawberries)
- 2 tbsp honey
- 1 tbsp chia seeds

Instructions:

1. Divide the Greek yogurt between two bowls.
2. Top each bowl with a generous portion of mixed berries.
3. Drizzle honey over the berries and yogurt.
4. Sprinkle chia seeds over the top for added texture and nutrition.
5. Serve immediately and enjoy.

Nutritional Data: Calories: 220 | Carbohydrates: 32g | Protein: 15g | Fat: 2.5g | Fiber: 4g

Wholesome Spinach and Feta Egg Muffins

⭐⭐⭐⭐⭐ | Preparation Time: 10 mins | Cooking Time: 20 mins | Portion Size: 6 muffins **Ingredients:**

- 4 large eggs
- 1/2 cup fresh spinach (chopped)
- 1/4 cup feta cheese (crumbled)
- 1/4 cup red bell pepper (diced)
- Salt and pepper to taste
- 1 tbsp olive oil

Instructions:

1. Preheat oven to 375°F (190°C) and grease a muffin tin.
2. In a bowl, whisk together the eggs, salt, and pepper.
3. Heat olive oil in a skillet and sauté the red bell pepper until slightly soft.
4. Add spinach to the skillet and cook until wilted.
5. Divide the spinach and bell pepper mixture among the muffin cups.
6. Pour the whisked eggs over the vegetables in each muffin cup.
7. Sprinkle crumbled feta cheese on top.
8. Bake for 20 minutes or until the eggs are set.
9. Allow to cool slightly before serving.

Nutritional Data: Calories: 90 | Carbohydrates: 1g | Protein: 6g | Fat: 7g | Fiber: 0.3g

Refreshing Berry and Kiwi Smoothie Bowl

⭐⭐⭐⭐⭐ | Preparation Time: 10 mins | Cooking Time: 0 mins | Portion Size: 2
Ingredients:

- 1 cup mixed berries (frozen)
- 2 ripe kiwis (peeled and sliced)
- 1 cup Greek yogurt (low-fat)
- 1/2 cup almond milk
- 2 tbsp chia seeds
- 1 tbsp honey

Instructions:

1. In a blender, combine the frozen berries, one kiwi, Greek yogurt, almond milk, and honey. Blend until smooth.
2. Pour the mixture into two bowls.
3. Top with slices of the remaining kiwi, a sprinkle of chia seeds, and additional berries if desired.
4. Serve immediately.

Nutritional Data: Calories: 190 | Carbohydrates: 32g | Protein: 9g | Fat: 4g | Fiber: 6g

Chia Seed and Coconut Overnight Pudding

⭐⭐⭐⭐⭐ | Preparation Time: 10 mins | Cooking Time: 0 mins (Chill overnight) | Portion Size: 2

Ingredients:

- 1/4 cup chia seeds
- 1 cup coconut milk
- 2 tbsp honey or maple syrup
- 1 tsp vanilla extract
- Fresh fruits for garnish

Instructions:

1. In a bowl, combine the chia seeds, coconut milk, honey, and vanilla extract. Stir well.
2. Divide the mixture between two jars or containers.
3. Cover and refrigerate overnight.
4. The next morning, stir the pudding well and top with your choice of fresh fruits.
5. Serve cold.

Nutritional Data: Calories: 280 | Carbohydrates: 30g | Protein: 4g | Fat: 17g | Fiber: 7g

---

Heartfelt Whole Grain Toast with Avocado and Tomato

★ ★ ★ ★ ★ | Preparation Time: 5 mins | Cooking Time: 2 mins | Portion Size: 2

Ingredients:

- 4 slices of whole grain bread
- 1 ripe avocado (sliced)
- 1 large tomato (sliced)
- Salt, pepper, and chili flakes to taste
- A drizzle of olive oil

Instructions:

1. Toast the whole grain bread slices until they're golden and crisp.
2. Arrange avocado slices and tomato slices on each toast.
3. Drizzle a bit of olive oil over the toppings.
4. Season with salt, pepper, and a sprinkle of chili flakes.
5. Serve immediately.

Nutritional Data: Calories: 250 | Carbohydrates: 30g | Protein: 8g | Fat: 12g | Fiber: 7g

---

Mango and Almond Butter Smoothie

★ ★ ★ ★ ★ | Preparation Time: 5 mins | Cooking Time: 0 mins | Portion Size: 2

Ingredients:

- 1 ripe mango (peeled and cubed)
- 2 tbsp almond butter
- 1 cup almond milk
- 1 tbsp honey or maple syrup
- A pinch of ground cinnamon

Instructions:

1. Combine mango, almond butter, almond milk, honey, and cinnamon in a blender.
2. Blend until smooth and creamy.
3. Pour into glasses and serve chilled.

Nutritional Data: Calories: 230 | Carbohydrates: 32g | Protein: 5g | Fat: 10g | Fiber: 4g

---

Hearty Oats and Apple Porridge

★ ★ ★ ★ ★ | Preparation Time: 5 mins | Cooking Time: 15 mins | Portion Size: 2

Ingredients:

- 1 cup rolled oats
- 2 cups almond milk or water
- 1 apple (cored and diced)
- 2 tbsp raisins or dried cranberries
- 1 tsp cinnamon
- 1 tbsp honey or maple syrup
- A pinch of salt

Instructions:

1. In a saucepan, bring the almond milk or water to a boil.
2. Add the rolled oats, diced apple, and a pinch of salt.
3. Reduce the heat and let it simmer, stirring occasionally for about 10 minutes or until oats are soft.
4. Stir in the cinnamon, raisins, and honey.
5. Serve hot, garnished with additional apple slices or a sprinkle of nuts.

Nutritional Data: Calories: 250 | Carbohydrates: 50g | Protein: 6g | Fat: 4g | Fiber: 7g

Heart-Healthy Breakfast Burrito

⭐⭐⭐⭐⭐ | Preparation Time: 10 mins | Cooking Time: 15 mins | Portion Size: 2 burritos

Ingredients:
- 2 whole grain tortillas
- 3 eggs (whisked)
- 1/2 cup black beans (cooked)
- 1/4 cup low-fat cheese (shredded)
- 1/4 cup salsa
- 1/4 cup bell peppers (diced)
- 1 tbsp olive oil
- Salt and pepper to taste

Instructions:
1. In a skillet, heat olive oil over medium heat. Add diced bell peppers and sauté until softened.
2. Add the whisked eggs to the skillet, stirring constantly until they are scrambled and cooked.
3. Lay out the whole grain tortillas on a flat surface.
4. Evenly distribute the scrambled eggs, black beans, cheese, and salsa in the center of each tortilla.
5. Fold the sides of the tortilla over the filling, then roll up from the bottom to form a burrito.
6. Serve immediately with additional salsa on the side, if desired.

Nutritional Data: Calories: 290 | Carbohydrates: 36g | Protein: 15g | Fat: 10g | Fiber: 6g

Zesty Lemon and Poppy Seed Pancakes

⭐⭐⭐⭐⭐ | Preparation Time: 10 mins | Cooking Time: 15 mins | Portion Size: 6 pancakes

Ingredients:

- 1 cup whole wheat flour
- 1 tbsp poppy seeds
- 1 tsp baking powder
- 1/4 tsp baking soda
- 1 cup buttermilk
- 1 egg
- 2 tbsp honey or maple syrup
- Zest of 1 lemon
- A pinch of salt
- Olive oil or non-stick cooking spray for the pan

Instructions:
1. In a large bowl, whisk together the flour, poppy seeds, baking powder, baking soda, and salt.
2. In another bowl, whisk together the buttermilk, egg, honey, and lemon zest.
3. Add the wet ingredients to the dry ingredients, stirring just until combined.
4. Heat a non-stick skillet over medium heat and lightly grease with oil or cooking spray.
5. Pour 1/4 cup of batter per pancake into the skillet.
6. Cook until bubbles appear on the surface, then flip and cook until the other side is golden brown.
7. Repeat with the remaining batter.
8. Serve warm with a drizzle of honey or a spoonful of Greek yogurt.

Nutritional Data: Calories: 150 | Carbohydrates: 28g | Protein: 5g | Fat: 3g | Fiber: 4g

Heartfelt Green Smoothie

⭐⭐⭐⭐⭐ | Preparation Time: 5 mins | Cooking Time: 0 mins | Portion Size: 2

Ingredients:
- 1 cup spinach or kale (washed)

- 1 banana (ripe)
- 1/2 cup pineapple chunks (fresh or frozen)
- 1 cup almond milk
- 1 tbsp chia seeds
- 1 tbsp honey or maple syrup (optional)

Instructions:

1. In a blender, combine the spinach or kale, banana, pineapple, almond milk, chia seeds, and sweetener if using.
2. Blend until smooth and creamy.
3. Pour into glasses and serve immediately.

Nutritional Data: Calories: 170 | Carbohydrates: 35g | Protein: 4g | Fat: 3g | Fiber: 6g

---

Fiber-Rich Muesli with Nuts and Seeds

⭐ ⭐ ⭐ ⭐ | Preparation Time: 5 mins | Cooking Time: 0 mins | Portion Size: 2

Ingredients:

- 1 cup rolled oats
- 1/4 cup mixed nuts (almonds, walnuts, cashews, chopped)
- 1/4 cup mixed seeds (sunflower, pumpkin, flaxseed)
- 1/4 cup dried fruits (raisins, apricots, chopped)
- 1 cup almond milk or Greek yogurt
- 1 tbsp honey or maple syrup

Instructions:

1. In a bowl, combine the rolled oats, nuts, seeds, and dried fruits.
2. Add the almond milk or Greek yogurt and mix well.
3. Drizzle with honey or maple syrup for added sweetness.
4. Let the mixture sit for 10 minutes to allow the oats to soften or refrigerate overnight for a chilled breakfast.
5. Serve in bowls, garnished with fresh fruits if desired.

Nutritional Data: Calories: 290 | Carbohydrates: 45g | Protein: 8g | Fat: 10g | Fiber: 7g

Grains, Legume

Quinoa Tabbouleh with Fresh Herbs

★ ★ ★ ★ ★ | Preparation Time: 15 mins | Cooking Time: 20 mins | Portion Size: 4

Ingredients:

- 1 cup quinoa (rinsed and drained)
- 2 cups water
- 1 cup fresh parsley (chopped)
- 1/2 cup fresh mint (chopped)
- 1 cup cherry tomatoes (halved)
- 1/2 cucumber (diced)
- 3 green onions (sliced)
- 3 tbsp olive oil
- Juice of 1 lemon
- Salt and pepper to taste

Instructions:

1. In a saucepan, bring water to a boil. Add quinoa and a pinch of salt. Reduce heat to low, cover, and simmer for 15-20 minutes or until quinoa is tender and the water is absorbed.
2. Fluff quinoa with a fork and allow it to cool.
3. In a large bowl, combine cooled quinoa, parsley, mint, cherry tomatoes, cucumber, and green onions.
4. In a separate small bowl, whisk together olive oil, lemon juice, salt, and pepper. Pour over the quinoa mixture and toss to combine.
5. Refrigerate for an hour before serving to let flavors meld.

Nutritional Data: Calories: 220 | Carbohydrates: 28g | Protein: 6g | Fat: 10g | Fiber: 3g

Mediterranean Chickpea Salad with Lemon Vinaigrette

★ ★ ★ ★ ★ | Preparation Time: 10 mins | Cooking Time: 0 mins | Portion Size: 4

Ingredients:

- 2 cups chickpeas (cooked and drained)
- 1 cup cherry tomatoes (quartered)
- 1/2 red onion (finely diced)
- 1/2 cucumber (diced)
- 1/4 cup Kalamata olives (pitted and halved)
- 1/4 cup feta cheese (crumbled)
- 1/4 cup fresh parsley (chopped)
- 3 tbsp olive oil
- Juice of 1 lemon
- 1 garlic clove (minced)
- Salt and pepper to taste

Instructions:

1. In a large bowl, combine chickpeas, cherry tomatoes, red onion, cucumber, olives, feta cheese, and parsley.
2. In a separate small bowl, whisk together olive oil, lemon juice, minced garlic, salt, and pepper. Pour over the salad and toss well to combine.
3. Serve immediately or refrigerate for later.

Nutritional Data: Calories: 290 | Carbohydrates: 35g | Protein: 10g | Fat: 13g | Fiber: 8g

Hearty Lentil and Vegetable Stew

★ ★ ★ ★ ★ | Preparation Time: 15 mins | Cooking Time: 40 mins | Portion Size: 6

Ingredients:

- 1 cup green lentils (rinsed and drained)
- 1 onion (chopped)
- 2 carrots (diced)
- 2 celery stalks (diced)
- 3 garlic cloves (minced)
- 1 can (14 oz) diced tomatoes (with juice)
- 6 cups vegetable broth
- 2 tsp cumin powder
- 1 tsp paprika
- 2 tbsp olive oil
- Salt and pepper to taste
- Fresh parsley for garnish

Instructions:

1. In a large pot, heat olive oil over medium heat. Add onions, carrots, and celery. Sauté until vegetables are softened.
2. Add minced garlic and sauté for another minute.
3. Stir in lentils, diced tomatoes with their juice, vegetable broth, cumin, paprika, salt, and pepper.
4. Bring the mixture to a boil, then reduce heat to low and let it simmer for 30-35 minutes or until lentils are tender.
5. Adjust seasoning if needed. Serve hot, garnished with fresh parsley.

Nutritional Data: Calories: 210 | Carbohydrates: 32g | Protein: 11g | Fat: 5g | Fiber: 14g

Barley Risotto with Mushrooms and Spinach

☆ ☆ ☆ ☆ ☆ | Preparation Time: 10 mins | Cooking Time: 45 mins | Portion Size: 4
Ingredients:
- 1 cup pearl barley (rinsed and drained)
- 1 onion (finely chopped)

- 2 garlic cloves (minced)
- 2 cups fresh mushrooms (sliced)
- 2 cups spinach (roughly chopped)
- 4 cups vegetable broth
- 2 tbsp olive oil
- Salt and pepper to taste
- Grated Parmesan cheese for garnish (optional)

Instructions:

1. In a deep pan, heat olive oil over medium heat. Add onions and sauté until translucent.
2. Add minced garlic and mushrooms, and sauté until mushrooms are golden.
3. Stir in the barley and cook for a couple of minutes.
4. Gradually pour in the vegetable broth, stirring continuously. Let the barley cook on a low flame, stirring occasionally until it's soft and has a creamy consistency.
5. Fold in the chopped spinach and cook until it's just wilted.
6. Season with salt and pepper. Serve hot with a sprinkle of Parmesan cheese if desired.

Nutritional Data:
Calories: 250 | Carbohydrates: 52g | Protein: 7g | Fat: 7g | Fiber: 11g

Chickpea and Spinach Curry

☆ ☆ ☆ ☆ ☆ | Preparation Time: 15 mins | Cooking Time: 30 mins | Portion Size: 4
Ingredients:
- 2 cups chickpeas (cooked and drained)
- 1 onion (chopped)
- 2 tomatoes (pureed)
- 2 cups spinach (chopped)
- 3 garlic cloves (minced)
- 1-inch ginger (grated)
- 2 tsp curry powder

- 1 tsp turmeric powder
- 1 tsp cumin seeds
- 2 tbsp coconut oil or olive oil
- Salt to taste

Instructions:

1. Heat oil in a pan, add cumin seeds and let them splutter.
2. Add onions and sauté until they turn translucent.
3. Add minced garlic and grated ginger, sauté for 2 minutes.
4. Pour in the tomato puree, curry powder, turmeric, and salt. Cook until the oil separates from the masala.
5. Add chickpeas and spinach. Mix well until everything is well coated with the masala.
6. Cover and simmer for 20 minutes. Serve warm with brown rice or whole-grain flatbread.

Nutritional Data:
Calories: 265 | Carbohydrates: 39g | Protein: 11g | Fat: 9g | Fiber: 10g

Bulgur Wheat and Roasted Vegetable Salad

✿ ✿ ✿ | Preparation Time: 15 mins | Cooking Time: 20 mins | Portion Size: 4

Ingredients:

- 1 cup bulgur wheat
- 2 bell peppers (diced)
- 1 zucchini (diced)
- 1 red onion (sliced)
- 2 tbsp olive oil
- Juice of 1 lemon
- 1/4 cup fresh parsley (chopped)
- Salt and pepper to taste

Instructions:

1. Preheat oven to 400°F (200°C).
2. Toss bell peppers, zucchini, and red onion in 1 tbsp of olive oil, salt, and pepper. Spread them on a baking sheet and roast for 20 minutes or until slightly charred.
3. While the veggies are roasting, boil 2 cups of water and add bulgur wheat. Cook on low heat until the water is absorbed and the bulgur is tender.
4. In a large bowl, combine roasted veggies and cooked bulgur. Drizzle with remaining olive oil, lemon juice, add chopped parsley, and toss to mix. Season with additional salt and pepper if needed.

Nutritional Data:
Calories: 220 | Carbohydrates: 41g | Protein: 6g | Fat: 7g | Fiber: 9g

Black Bean and Quinoa Stuffed Peppers

✿ ✿ ✿ ✿ | Preparation Time: 20 mins | Cooking Time: 35 mins | Portion Size: 4

Ingredients:

- 4 large bell peppers (any color)
- 1 cup cooked quinoa
- 1 cup black beans (cooked and drained)
- 1 cup corn kernels
- 1/2 cup tomato salsa
- 1 tsp cumin powder
- 1 tsp paprika
- Salt and pepper to taste
- 2 tbsp olive oil
- Fresh cilantro for garnish

Instructions:

1. Preheat oven to 375°F (190°C).
2. Cut off the tops of the bell peppers and remove the seeds and membranes.

3. In a large mixing bowl, combine quinoa, black beans, corn, salsa, cumin, paprika, salt, and pepper.
4. Stuff each bell pepper with the quinoa mixture.
5. Place the stuffed peppers in a baking dish. Drizzle with olive oil.
6. Cover with aluminum foil and bake for 30-35 minutes or until the peppers are tender.
7. Serve hot, garnished with fresh cilantro.

Nutritional Data:
Calories: 265 | Carbohydrates: 44g | Protein: 10g | Fat: 7g | Fiber: 8g

---

Creamy Butternut Squash and Lentil Soup

⭐ ⭐ ⭐ ⭐ ⭐ | Preparation Time: 15 mins | Cooking Time: 40 mins | Portion Size: 6
Ingredients:
- 1 medium butternut squash (peeled, seeded, and cubed)
- 1 cup green lentils (rinsed and drained)
- 1 onion (diced)
- 2 garlic cloves (minced)
- 4 cups vegetable broth
- 1 can (14 oz) coconut milk
- 2 tsp curry powder
- 2 tbsp olive oil
- Salt and pepper to taste

Instructions:
1. In a large pot, heat olive oil over medium heat. Add onions and sauté until translucent.
2. Add minced garlic and curry powder, stirring for another minute.
3. Add butternut squash cubes, lentils, and vegetable broth. Bring to a boil.

4. Lower the heat, cover, and simmer for 25-30 minutes or until the squash and lentils are tender.
5. Use an immersion blender (or a regular blender in batches) to blend the soup until smooth.
6. Stir in coconut milk and season with salt and pepper. Heat for another 5 minutes.
7. Serve warm with crusty whole-grain bread.

Nutritional Data:
Calories: 320 | Carbohydrates: 46g | Protein: 13g | Fat: 11g | Fiber: 12g

---

Millet and Veggie Stir-Fry with Tamari Glaze

⭐ ⭐ ⭐ ⭐ ⭐ | Preparation Time: 15 mins | Cooking Time: 25 mins | Portion Size: 4
Ingredients:
- 1 cup millet (rinsed and drained)
- 2 cups water
- 1 bell pepper (sliced)
- 1 zucchini (sliced into half-moons)
- 1 carrot (julienned)
- 2 green onions (sliced)
- 3 tbsp tamari or soy sauce
- 1 tbsp sesame oil
- 2 tbsp olive oil
- 1 tsp ginger (grated)
- 1 garlic clove (minced)
- 1 tbsp sesame seeds (optional)

Instructions:
1. In a saucepan, bring water to a boil. Add millet, reduce heat to low, cover, and cook for about 20 minutes or until all water is absorbed. Fluff with a fork.
2. In a wok or large pan, heat olive oil. Add ginger and garlic and sauté for a minute.

3. Add bell pepper, zucchini, and carrot. Stir-fry for about 5 minutes or until veggies are slightly tender.
4. Stir in the cooked millet, tamari, and sesame oil. Mix well.
5. Serve hot, garnished with green onions and sesame seeds.

Nutritional Data:
Calories: 275 | Carbohydrates: 41g | Protein: 7g | Fat: 10g | Fiber: 6g

---

Red Lentil Dahl with Spinach

☆ ☆ ☆ ☆ | Preparation Time: 15 mins | Cooking Time: 30 mins | Portion Size: 4
Ingredients:
- 1 cup red lentils (rinsed and drained)
- 1 onion (diced)
- 2 garlic cloves (minced)
- 1-inch ginger (grated)
- 2 cups spinach (roughly chopped)
- 2 tomatoes (chopped)
- 2 tsp curry powder
- 1 tsp turmeric powder
- 2 tbsp coconut oil or olive oil
- 4 cups water
- Salt to taste
- Fresh cilantro for garnish

Instructions:
1. Heat oil in a pot, add onions, and sauté until they turn translucent.
2. Add garlic and ginger, sautéing for another 2 minutes.
3. Stir in the curry powder, turmeric, and tomatoes. Cook until the tomatoes are soft.
4. Add the red lentils and water. Bring to a boil.
5. Lower the heat and simmer until lentils are tender, around 20 minutes.

6. Fold in the spinach and cook just until wilted.
7. Season with salt and garnish with fresh cilantro before serving.

Nutritional Data:
Calories: 280 | Carbohydrates: 45g | Protein: 15g | Fat: 5g | Fiber: 15g

---

Buckwheat Groats with Sautéed Veggies

☆ ☆ ☆ ☆ | Preparation Time: 10 mins | Cooking Time: 20 mins | Portion Size: 4
Ingredients:
- 1 cup buckwheat groats
- 2 cups water
- 1 zucchini (diced)
- 1 red bell pepper (diced)
- 1/2 cup cherry tomatoes (halved)
- 2 tbsp olive oil
- 2 garlic cloves (minced)
- Salt and pepper to taste
- Fresh parsley (chopped for garnish)

Instructions:
1. Bring water to a boil in a saucepan, add buckwheat groats, lower the heat, and simmer covered for about 10 minutes or until all the water is absorbed.
2. In a separate pan, heat olive oil. Add garlic and sauté until fragrant.
3. Add zucchini and bell pepper, sautéing for about 5 minutes.
4. Stir in cherry tomatoes and cook for another 3 minutes.
5. Combine the veggies with the cooked buckwheat groats. Season with salt, pepper, and garnish with fresh parsley.

Nutritional Data:
Calories: 225 | Carbohydrates: 38g | Protein: 8g | Fat: 7g | Fiber: 5g

Spiced Chickpea and Farro Bowl

★ ★ ★ ★ ★ | Preparation Time: 15 mins | Cooking Time: 25 mins | Portion Size: 4

Ingredients:
- 1 cup farro (rinsed and drained)
- 3 cups water
- 1 can (15 oz) chickpeas (rinsed and drained)
- 2 tsp paprika
- 1 tsp cumin powder
- 1 tbsp olive oil
- Salt and pepper to taste
- 1/2 cucumber (diced)
- 1/2 red onion (sliced)
- Fresh cilantro for garnish

Instructions:
1. In a saucepan, bring water to a boil. Add farro, reduce heat, and simmer covered for about 25 minutes or until tender. Drain any excess water.
2. In a pan, heat olive oil. Add chickpeas, paprika, cumin, salt, and pepper. Sauté until the chickpeas are well coated and heated through.
3. Combine cooked farro, spiced chickpeas, cucumber, and red onion in a bowl. Garnish with fresh cilantro.

Nutritional Data:
Calories: 310 | Carbohydrates: 58g | Protein: 12g | Fat: 5g | Fiber: 10g

Mung Bean and Rice Pilaf

★ ★ ★ ★ | Preparation Time: 15 mins | Cooking Time: 35 mins | Portion Size: 4

Ingredients:
- 1 cup mung beans (soaked for 2 hours)
- 1 cup brown rice
- 1 onion (diced)
- 2 garlic cloves (minced)
- 4 cups vegetable broth
- 2 tsp turmeric powder
- 1 tsp cumin seeds
- 2 tbsp olive oil
- Salt to taste
- Fresh coriander leaves for garnish

Instructions:
1. In a large pot, heat olive oil. Add cumin seeds and allow them to sizzle.
2. Add onions and sauté until translucent.
3. Stir in garlic and cook for another minute.
4. Add the drained mung beans, rice, turmeric, and salt. Mix well.
5. Pour in the vegetable broth and bring the mixture to a boil.
6. Reduce heat to low, cover, and simmer for 30-35 minutes, or until both rice and mung beans are cooked through.
7. Garnish with fresh coriander leaves before serving.

Nutritional Data:
Calories: 340 | Carbohydrates: 65g | Protein: 14g | Fat: 6g | Fiber: 8g

Spelt Berry Salad with Roasted Veggies

★ ★ ★ ★ ★ | Preparation Time: 15 mins | Cooking Time: 40 mins | Portion Size: 4

Ingredients:
- 1 cup spelt berries
- 3 cups water
- 1 zucchini (sliced)
- 1 red bell pepper (diced)
- 1/2 cup cherry tomatoes (halved)
- 2 tbsp olive oil
- 2 tbsp balsamic vinegar
- Salt and pepper to taste
- Fresh basil leaves (chopped for garnish)

Instructions:

1. Preheat the oven to 400°F (200°C).
2. Toss the zucchini, bell pepper, and cherry tomatoes in 1 tbsp of olive oil. Season with salt and pepper.
3. Spread the vegetables on a baking sheet and roast for 20-25 minutes or until tender.
4. Meanwhile, bring water to a boil in a saucepan. Add spelt berries, reduce heat, and simmer covered for about 30 minutes or until tender. Drain any excess water.
5. Combine the roasted vegetables and spelt berries in a bowl. Drizzle with the remaining olive oil and balsamic vinegar. Garnish with fresh basil.

Nutritional Data:
Calories: 260 | Carbohydrates: 45g | Protein: 9g | Fat: 7g | Fiber: 8g

---

Barley and Lentil Soup with Kale

☆ ☆ ☆ ☆ | Preparation Time: 15 mins | Cooking Time: 45 mins | Portion Size: 6

Ingredients:

- 1 cup barley
- 1/2 cup green lentils
- 1 onion (diced)
- 2 carrots (diced)
- 2 celery stalks (diced)
- 2 garlic cloves (minced)
- 4 cups vegetable broth
- 2 cups water
- 2 cups kale (chopped)
- 2 tbsp olive oil
- Salt and pepper to taste

Instructions:

1. Heat olive oil in a large pot. Add onions, carrots, and celery. Sauté until onions are translucent.

2. Add garlic and cook for another minute.
3. Pour in the vegetable broth, water, barley, and lentils. Bring to a boil.
4. Reduce the heat to low, cover, and simmer for about 35 minutes.
5. Once barley and lentils are almost cooked, stir in the chopped kale and cook for an additional 10 minutes.
6. Season with salt and pepper. Serve hot.

Nutritional Data:
Calories: 280 | Carbohydrates: 52g | Protein: 10g | Fat: 5g | Fiber: 11g

---

Quinoa and Black Bean Tacos

☆ ☆ ☆ ☆ | Preparation Time: 10 mins | Cooking Time: 25 mins | Portion Size: 4

Ingredients:

- 1 cup quinoa (rinsed and drained)
- 2 cups vegetable broth
- 1 can (15 oz) black beans (rinsed and drained)
- 1 bell pepper (diced)
- 1 onion (diced)
- 2 garlic cloves (minced)
- 2 tbsp olive oil
- 1 tsp ground cumin
- 8 small whole grain tortillas
- Fresh cilantro, salsa, and avocado for garnish
- Salt and pepper to taste

Instructions:

1. In a pot, combine quinoa and vegetable broth. Bring to a boil, then reduce heat, cover, and simmer for about 20 minutes, or until quinoa is cooked.
2. In a skillet, heat olive oil over medium heat. Add onion and bell pepper, sautéing until softened.

3. Add garlic, cumin, and black beans. Cook for another 5 minutes.

4. Mix in the cooked quinoa and season with salt and pepper.

5. Warm the tortillas. Scoop the quinoa and black bean mixture onto each tortilla. Top with salsa, fresh cilantro, and avocado slices.

Nutritional Data:

Calories: 450 | Carbohydrates: 75g | Protein: 15g | Fat: 10g | Fiber: 13g

Black-Eyed Peas Salad with Avocado

☆ ☆ ☆ ☆ | Preparation Time: 15 mins | Cooking Time: 0 mins | Portion Size: 4

Ingredients:

- 1 can (15 oz) black-eyed peas (rinsed and drained)
- 1 avocado (diced)
- 1 red bell pepper (diced)
- 1/2 red onion (sliced)
- 2 tbsp cilantro (chopped)
- 2 tbsp olive oil
- 1 tbsp lime juice
- Salt and pepper to taste

Instructions:

1. In a large bowl, combine black-eyed peas, avocado, bell pepper, onion, and cilantro.

2. In a separate small bowl, whisk together olive oil, lime juice, salt, and pepper.

3. Drizzle the dressing over the salad ingredients and gently toss to combine.

Nutritional Data:

Calories: 290 | Carbohydrates: 38g | Protein: 11g | Fat: 12g | Fiber: 10g

Chickpea Flour Pancakes with Spinach

☆ ☆ ☆ ☆ | Preparation Time: 10 mins | Cooking Time: 20 mins | Portion Size: 4

Ingredients:

- 1 cup chickpea flour
- 1 1/2 cups water
- 2 cups spinach (chopped)
- 1/2 red onion (finely chopped)
- 1/4 tsp turmeric powder
- Salt to taste
- Olive oil for cooking

Instructions:

1. In a bowl, whisk together chickpea flour, water, turmeric, and salt to create a smooth batter.

2. Stir in the chopped spinach and red onion.

3. Heat a little olive oil in a non-stick pan over medium heat. Pour a ladle of the batter to form a pancake. Cook until bubbles appear on the surface, then flip and cook the other side.

4. Repeat with the remaining batter. Serve warm.

Nutritional Data:

Calories: 150 | Carbohydrates: 23g | Protein: 8g | Fat: 3g | Fiber: 4g

Millet and Roasted Vegetable Salad

☆ ☆ ☆ ☆ ☆ | Preparation Time: 15 mins | Cooking Time: 25 mins | Portion Size: 4

Ingredients:

- 1 cup millet
- 2 cups water
- 1 zucchini (sliced)
- 1 bell pepper (sliced)
- 1/2 red onion (sliced)
- 2 tbsp olive oil (divided)

- 2 tbsp balsamic vinegar
- Salt and pepper to taste

Instructions:

1. Preheat the oven to 400°F (200°C).
2. Toss zucchini, bell pepper, and red onion in 1 tbsp of olive oil. Spread on a baking tray and roast for about 20 minutes or until tender.
3. While the veggies are roasting, bring water to a boil in a saucepan. Add millet, reduce heat, cover, and simmer for about 20 minutes or until the water is absorbed.
4. In a large bowl, combine cooked millet and roasted veggies. Drizzle with remaining olive oil and balsamic vinegar. Season with salt and pepper.

Nutritional Data:

Calories: 260 | Carbohydrates: 42g | Protein: 6g | Fat: 8g | Fiber: 5g

---

Buckwheat Risotto with Mushrooms and Spinach

| Preparation Time: 10 mins | Cooking Time: 35 mins | Portion Size: 4

Ingredients:

- 1 cup buckwheat groats
- 4 cups vegetable broth
- 1 cup sliced mushrooms
- 2 cups fresh spinach
- 1 onion (finely chopped)
- 2 garlic cloves (minced)
- 2 tbsp olive oil
- 1/4 cup grated Parmesan (optional for a vegan version)
- Salt and pepper to taste

Instructions:

1. In a large saucepan, heat olive oil over medium heat. Add the onion and sauté until translucent.

2. Add garlic and mushrooms, cooking until mushrooms have softened.
3. Pour in buckwheat groats, stirring constantly for about 2 minutes.
4. Gradually add the vegetable broth, one cup at a time, allowing each addition to be absorbed before adding the next. This process should take around 30 minutes.
5. Once the buckwheat is tender and creamy, fold in the spinach and cook until wilted.
6. Season with salt and pepper. Stir in the Parmesan, if using.

Nutritional Data:

Calories: 290 | Carbohydrates: 50g | Protein: 11g | Fat: 7g | Fiber: 7g

---

Lentil Stuffed Bell Peppers

| Preparation Time: 15 mins | Cooking Time: 45 mins | Portion Size: 4

Ingredients:

- 4 large bell peppers (any color)
- 1 cup cooked lentils
- 1 onion (chopped)
- 2 garlic cloves (minced)
- 1 cup diced tomatoes (canned or fresh)
- 2 tbsp olive oil
- 1 tsp dried oregano
- Salt and pepper to taste
- Fresh parsley for garnish

Instructions:

1. Preheat the oven to 375°F (190°C).
2. Slice off the tops of the bell peppers and remove the seeds.
3. In a skillet, heat olive oil and sauté onions until translucent. Add garlic and cook for another minute.
4. Stir in diced tomatoes, oregano, salt, and pepper. Simmer for 5 minutes.

5. Remove from heat and mix in the cooked lentils.
6. Stuff each bell pepper with the lentil mixture and place in a baking dish.
7. Cover with foil and bake for about 35-40 minutes, until peppers are tender.
8. Garnish with fresh parsley before serving.

Nutritional Data:
Calories: 220 | Carbohydrates: 35g | Protein: 10g | Fat: 6g | Fiber: 10g

Sorghum Salad with Mixed Veggies

⭐⭐⭐⭐ | Preparation Time: 15 mins | Cooking Time: 50 mins | Portion Size: 4

Ingredients:
- 1 cup sorghum
- 3 cups water
- 1 cup cherry tomatoes (halved)
- 1 cucumber (diced)
- 1 carrot (shredded)
- 1/4 cup fresh basil (chopped)
- 2 tbsp olive oil
- 1 tbsp lemon juice
- Salt and pepper to taste

Instructions:
1. Rinse sorghum under cold water.
2. In a pot, bring water to a boil. Add sorghum, reduce the heat to low, cover, and simmer for about 50 minutes or until tender.
3. Once cooked, drain any excess water and let it cool.
4. In a large bowl, combine cooled sorghum, cherry tomatoes, cucumber, carrot, and basil.
5. Drizzle with olive oil and lemon juice. Toss to combine. Season with salt and pepper.

Nutritional Data:
Calories: 240 | Carbohydrates: 47g | Protein: 6g | Fat: 7g | Fiber: 6g

Chia Seeds and Oats Porridge

⭐⭐⭐⭐ | Preparation Time: 5 mins | Cooking Time: 10 mins | Portion Size: 2

Ingredients:
- 1/2 cup rolled oats
- 2 tbsp chia seeds
- 1 1/2 cups almond milk (or any preferred milk)
- 1 banana (sliced)
- 1 tsp honey or maple syrup
- 1/4 tsp vanilla extract
- Fresh berries for garnish

Instructions:
1. In a saucepan, combine rolled oats, chia seeds, and almond milk. Bring to a simmer.
2. Reduce the heat and cook for about 8-10 minutes, stirring occasionally, until the oats are soft and have absorbed the milk.
3. Remove from heat and stir in the banana slices, honey, and vanilla extract.
4. Serve in bowls, garnished with fresh berries.

Nutritional Data:
Calories: 260 | Carbohydrates: 44g | Protein: 7g | Fat: 8g | Fiber: 10g

Farro and Roasted Beet Salad

⭐⭐⭐⭐ | Preparation Time: 10 mins | Cooking Time: 40 mins | Portion Size: 4

Ingredients:
- 1 cup farro
- 3 cups water

- 3 medium beets (peeled and diced)
- 2 tbsp olive oil (divided)
- 1/4 cup feta cheese (crumbled)
- 2 tbsp fresh dill (chopped)
- 2 tbsp lemon juice
- Salt and pepper to taste

Instructions:

1. Preheat the oven to 400°F (200°C).
2. Toss beets in 1 tbsp olive oil, season with salt, and spread on a baking sheet. Roast for about 30 minutes or until tender.
3. Meanwhile, in a saucepan, bring water to a boil. Add farro, reduce heat, and simmer for about 30 minutes, or until the farro is tender. Drain excess water and let it cool.
4. In a large bowl, combine cooled farro, roasted beets, feta, and dill.
5. Drizzle with the remaining olive oil and lemon juice. Toss to combine. Season with salt and pepper.

Nutritional Data:
Calories: 320 | Carbohydrates: 54g | Protein: 9g | Fat: 9g | Fiber: 8g

Spelt Pasta with Lentil Bolognese

✦ ✦ ✦ ✦ ✦ | Preparation Time: 15 mins | Cooking Time: 40 mins | Portion Size: 4

Ingredients:

- 2 cups spelt pasta
- 1 cup cooked lentils
- 1 can (15 oz) crushed tomatoes
- 1 onion (chopped)
- 2 garlic cloves (minced)
- 1 carrot (chopped)
- 1 celery stalk (chopped)
- 2 tbsp olive oil
- 1 tsp dried basil
- Salt and pepper to taste

- Fresh parsley for garnish

Instructions:

1. Cook spelt pasta according to package instructions. Drain and set aside.
2. In a large saucepan, heat olive oil over medium heat. Add onion, carrot, and celery. Cook until softened.
3. Add garlic and cook for another minute.
4. Pour in crushed tomatoes, cooked lentils, dried basil, salt, and pepper. Let it simmer for about 30 minutes.
5. Serve the lentil Bolognese over the spelt pasta. Garnish with fresh parsley.

Nutritional Data:
Calories: 350 | Carbohydrates: 60g | Protein: 15g | Fat: 7g | Fiber: 11g

Bulgur Wheat and Veggie Stir-Fry

✦ ✦ ✦ ✦ ✦ | Preparation Time: 15 mins | Cooking Time: 20 mins | Portion Size: 4

Ingredients:

- 1 cup bulgur wheat
- 2 cups water
- 1 bell pepper (sliced)
- 1 zucchini (sliced)
- 1 carrot (julienned)
- 2 garlic cloves (minced)
- 2 tbsp soy sauce
- 1 tbsp olive oil
- 1 tsp sesame seeds
- Green onions for garnish

Instructions:

1. In a pot, bring water to a boil. Add bulgur wheat, reduce heat, cover, and simmer for about 15 minutes or until the water is absorbed. Set aside.
2. In a wok or large skillet, heat olive oil over medium-high heat. Add bell pepper, zucchini, and carrot. Stir-fry for about 5 minutes.

3. Add garlic and stir-fry for another minute.
4. Add the cooked bulgur wheat and soy sauce. Toss everything to combine.
5. Serve in bowls, garnished with sesame seeds and sliced green onions.

Nutritional Data:
Calories: 230 | Carbohydrates: 47g | Protein: 7g | Fat: 4g | Fiber: 9g

Sides and Vegetables

Roasted Brussels Sprouts with Garlic & Lemon

☆☆☆☆☆ | Preparation Time: 10 mins | Cooking Time: 25 mins | Portion Size: 4

Ingredients:

400g Brussels sprouts (trimmed and halved)

2 tbsp olive oil

4 garlic cloves (minced)

Zest and juice of 1 lemon

Salt and pepper to taste

Instructions:

Preheat the oven to 400°F (200°C).

In a mixing bowl, toss the Brussels sprouts with olive oil, minced garlic, lemon zest, salt, and pepper.

Spread them on a baking sheet in a single layer.

Roast for about 20-25 minutes or until golden brown and crispy.

Before serving, drizzle with fresh lemon juice.

Nutritional Data:

Calories: 120 | Carbohydrates: 15g | Protein: 4g | Fat: 6g | Fiber: 5g

Quinoa-Stuffed Bell Peppers

☆☆☆☆☆ | Preparation Time: 15 mins | Cooking Time: 30 mins | Portion Size: 4

Ingredients:

4 large bell peppers (tops removed and deseeded)

1 cup cooked quinoa

1 cup cherry tomatoes (halved)

1/2 cup feta cheese (crumbled)

2 tbsp fresh basil (chopped)

1 tbsp olive oil

Salt and pepper to taste

Instructions:

Preheat the oven to 375°F (190°C).

In a bowl, combine cooked quinoa, cherry tomatoes, feta cheese, basil, olive oil, salt, and pepper.

Stuff each bell pepper with the quinoa mixture, pressing down gently to pack the filling.

Place the stuffed peppers in a baking dish.

Bake for about 30 minutes or until the peppers are tender.

Serve warm.

Nutritional Data:

Calories: 220 | Carbohydrates: 28g | Protein: 8g | Fat: 9g | Fiber: 5g

Garlic Steamed Green Beans with Almonds

☆☆☆☆☆ | Preparation Time: 10 mins | Cooking Time: 10 mins | Portion Size: 4

Ingredients:

400g green beans (trimmed)

2 tbsp olive oil

4 garlic cloves (minced)

1/4 cup almonds (sliced)

Salt to taste

Instructions:

In a large pot, bring water to a boil. Add green beans and steam for 5 minutes or until tender but crisp.

In a skillet, heat olive oil over medium heat. Add minced garlic and cook until aromatic.

Add steamed green beans and almonds to the skillet. Toss to coat the beans with garlic and oil.

Season with salt and serve warm.

Nutritional Data:
Calories: 120 | Carbohydrates: 10g | Protein: 4g | Fat: 8g | Fiber: 4g

Zucchini & Tomato Gratin with Olive Crumble

⭐⭐⭐⭐⭐ | Preparation Time: 15 mins | Cooking Time: 25 mins | Portion Size: 4

Ingredients:

2 zucchinis (sliced)

2 tomatoes (sliced)

1/4 cup black olives (chopped)

1/4 cup breadcrumbs

2 tbsp olive oil

1 garlic clove (minced)

Salt and pepper to taste

Instructions:

Preheat the oven to 375°F (190°C).

In a baking dish, layer slices of zucchini and tomato alternately.

In a bowl, mix olives, breadcrumbs, olive oil, minced garlic, salt, and pepper to form a crumbly mixture.

Sprinkle this olive crumble over the zucchini and tomato layers.

Bake for 25 minutes or until the top is golden and crispy.

Serve warm.

Nutritional Data:
Calories: 140 | Carbohydrates: 12g | Protein: 3g | Fat: 9g | Fiber: 3g

Balsamic-Glazed Roasted Root Vegetables

⭐⭐⭐⭐⭐ | Preparation Time: 15 mins | Cooking Time: 40 mins | Portion Size: 4

Ingredients:

200g carrots (peeled and sliced)

200g parsnips (peeled and sliced)

200g turnips (peeled and cubed)

3 tbsp olive oil

2 tbsp balsamic vinegar

1 tbsp fresh rosemary (chopped)

Salt and pepper to taste

Instructions:

Preheat the oven to 400°F (200°C).

In a large bowl, toss the vegetables with olive oil, balsamic vinegar, rosemary, salt, and pepper.

Spread the vegetables on a baking sheet in a single layer.

Roast for about 35-40 minutes, turning once, until tender and slightly caramelized.

Serve warm.

Nutritional Data:
Calories: 180 | Carbohydrates: 25g | Protein: 2g | Fat: 8g | Fiber: 6g

Turmeric Cauliflower Steaks

⭐⭐⭐⭐⭐ | Preparation Time: 10 mins | Cooking Time: 25 mins | Portion Size: 4

Ingredients:

1 large cauliflower head (sliced into 1-inch thick steaks)

2 tbsp olive oil

1 tsp turmeric powder

Salt and pepper to taste

Instructions:

Preheat the oven to 400°F (200°C).

Place the cauliflower steaks on a baking sheet.

Brush both sides of each steak with olive oil and sprinkle with turmeric, salt, and pepper.

Roast for 25 minutes, turning once, until tender and golden.

Serve immediately.

Nutritional Data:
Calories: 100 | Carbohydrates: 8g | Protein: 3g | Fat: 7g | Fiber: 3g

Mediterranean Spinach & Chickpea Salad

☆☆☆☆☆ | Preparation Time: 15 mins | Cooking Time: 0 mins | Portion Size: 4

Ingredients:

4 cups fresh spinach (washed and chopped)

1 can chickpeas (drained and rinsed)

1/2 cup cherry tomatoes (halved)

1/4 cup red onion (sliced)

1/4 cup feta cheese (crumbled)

2 tbsp olive oil

1 tbsp lemon juice

Salt and pepper to taste

Instructions:

In a large bowl, combine spinach, chickpeas, tomatoes, and red onion.

In a small bowl, whisk together olive oil, lemon juice, salt, and pepper to make the dressing.

Pour the dressing over the salad and toss to combine.

Top with crumbled feta cheese before serving.

Nutritional Data:

Calories: 210 | Carbohydrates: 20g | Protein: 8g | Fat: 11g | Fiber: 6g

Lemon-Parsley Asparagus Spears

☆☆☆☆☆ | Preparation Time: 10 mins | Cooking Time: 10 mins | Portion Size: 4

Ingredients:

400g asparagus spears (trimmed)

2 tbsp olive oil

Zest and juice of 1 lemon

2 tbsp fresh parsley (chopped)

Salt and pepper to taste

Instructions:

In a large skillet, heat olive oil over medium heat.

Add the asparagus and cook, turning occasionally, for 7-10 minutes or until tender and slightly charred.

Remove from heat and toss with lemon zest, lemon juice, parsley, salt, and pepper.

Serve immediately.

Nutritional Data:

Calories: 90 | Carbohydrates: 7g | Protein: 3g | Fat: 7g | Fiber: 3g

Olive Oil Whipped Sweet Potatoes

☆☆☆☆☆ | Preparation Time: 15 mins | Cooking Time: 30 mins | Portion Size: 4

Ingredients:

4 medium sweet potatoes (peeled and cubed)

3 tbsp olive oil

1/4 cup unsweetened almond milk

Salt and pepper to taste

Instructions:

In a large pot, bring water to a boil. Add the sweet potato cubes and cook until fork-tender, about 20 minutes.

Drain the water and transfer the sweet potatoes to a mixing bowl.

Add olive oil and almond milk, then whip using a hand mixer or potato masher until smooth.

Season with salt and pepper. Serve warm.

Nutritional Data:

Calories: 230 | Carbohydrates: 40g | Protein: 3g | Fat: 7g | Fiber: 6g

Stir-Fried Snow Peas with Sesame Seeds

☆☆☆☆☆ | Preparation Time: 10 mins | Cooking Time: 10 mins | Portion Size: 4

Ingredients:

400g snow peas (trimmed)

1 tbsp sesame oil

1 tbsp toasted sesame seeds

2 garlic cloves (minced)

Salt to taste

Instructions:

Heat sesame oil in a wok or large skillet over medium-high heat.

Add garlic and sauté until aromatic.

Add snow peas and stir-fry for about 5 minutes or until vibrant and slightly tender.

Sprinkle with toasted sesame seeds and salt. Toss to combine and serve immediately.

Nutritional Data:

Calories: 80 | Carbohydrates: 7g | Protein: 3g | Fat: 5g | Fiber: 2g

Kale, Cranberry, and Quinoa Salad

☆ ☆ ☆ ☆ ☆ | Preparation Time: 15 mins | Cooking Time: 20 mins | Portion Size: 4

Ingredients:

2 cups kale (destemmed and chopped)

1 cup cooked quinoa

1/2 cup dried cranberries

1/4 cup pumpkin seeds

2 tbsp olive oil

1 tbsp apple cider vinegar

Salt and pepper to taste

Instructions:

In a large bowl, combine kale, quinoa, cranberries, and pumpkin seeds.

In a small bowl, whisk together olive oil, apple cider vinegar, salt, and pepper to create the dressing.

Pour the dressing over the salad, toss to combine, and serve.

Nutritional Data:

Calories: 240 | Carbohydrates: 33g | Protein: 6g | Fat: 10g | Fiber: 4g

Baked Eggplant & Tomato Casserole

☆ ☆ ☆ ☆ | Preparation Time: 15 mins | Cooking Time: 35 mins | Portion Size: 4

Ingredients:

1 large eggplant (sliced)

4 tomatoes (sliced)

1/4 cup grated Parmesan cheese

2 tbsp olive oil

2 garlic cloves (minced)

1 tsp dried oregano

Salt and pepper to taste

Instructions:

Preheat the oven to 375°F (190°C).

In a baking dish, alternate layers of eggplant and tomato slices.

In a small bowl, combine olive oil, minced garlic, oregano, salt, and pepper. Drizzle this mixture over the layered vegetables.

Sprinkle grated Parmesan cheese on top.

Bake for 35 minutes or until the vegetables are tender and the cheese is golden brown. Serve warm.

Nutritional Data:

Calories: 160 | Carbohydrates: 15g | Protein: 6g | Fat: 9g | Fiber: 6g

Brussels Sprouts with Lemon and Pine Nuts

☆ ☆ ☆ ☆ | Preparation Time: 15 mins | Cooking Time: 15 mins | Portion Size: 4

Ingredients:

400g Brussels sprouts (trimmed and halved)

2 tbsp olive oil

Zest and juice of 1 lemon

1/4 cup pine nuts

Salt and pepper to taste

Instructions:

In a large skillet, heat the olive oil over medium heat.

Add the Brussels sprouts and sauté until they begin to turn golden brown, about 8-10 minutes.

Add the pine nuts and continue to sauté until they're toasted.

Remove from heat, and toss with lemon zest, lemon juice, salt, and pepper. Serve warm.

Nutritional Data:

Calories: 170 | Carbohydrates: 12g | Protein: 5g | Fat: 13g | Fiber: 4g

Zucchini Ribbons with Pesto and Cherry Tomatoes

⭐⭐⭐⭐⭐ | Preparation Time: 20 mins | Cooking Time: 5 mins | Portion Size: 4

Ingredients:

2 large zucchinis

1 cup cherry tomatoes (halved)

1/4 cup homemade pesto

2 tbsp olive oil

Salt and pepper to taste

Instructions:

Using a vegetable peeler, create long, thin ribbons from the zucchinis.

In a large skillet, heat olive oil over medium-high heat.

Add zucchini ribbons and sauté for 2-3 minutes or just until tender.

Remove from heat and toss with pesto and cherry tomatoes. Season with salt and pepper, and serve immediately.

Nutritional Data:

Calories: 140 | Carbohydrates: 6g | Protein: 3g | Fat: 12g | Fiber: 2g

Chili Lime Roasted Broccoli

⭐⭐⭐⭐⭐ | Preparation Time: 10 mins | Cooking Time: 20 mins | Portion Size: 4

Ingredients:

400g broccoli florets

2 tbsp olive oil

Zest and juice of 1 lime

1 tsp chili powder

Salt and pepper to taste

Instructions:

Preheat the oven to 425°F (220°C).

In a large bowl, toss the broccoli florets with olive oil, lime zest, lime juice, chili powder, salt, and pepper.

Spread the broccoli on a baking sheet in a single layer.

Roast for about 15-20 minutes or until the edges of the broccoli are crispy and browned. Serve hot.

Nutritional Data:

Calories: 110 | Carbohydrates: 8g | Protein: 3g | Fat: 8g | Fiber: 3g

Garlic Green Beans Almondine

⭐⭐⭐⭐⭐ | Preparation Time: 10 mins | Cooking Time: 15 mins | Portion Size: 4

Ingredients:

400g green beans (trimmed)

2 tbsp olive oil

3 garlic cloves (minced)

1/4 cup sliced almonds

Salt and pepper to taste

Instructions:

In a large skillet, heat the olive oil over medium heat.

Add the garlic and sauté until aromatic.

Add the green beans and continue to cook for about 8-10 minutes, stirring occasionally, until the beans are tender-crisp.

Add the sliced almonds and continue to sauté until they are golden brown.

Season with salt and pepper and serve immediately.

Nutritional Data:
Calories: 130 | Carbohydrates: 9g | Protein: 4g | Fat: 10g | Fiber: 4g

Rosemary Roasted Carrots

⭐⭐⭐⭐⭐ | Preparation Time: 10 mins | Cooking Time: 25 mins | Portion Size: 4

Ingredients:

400g carrots (peeled and halved lengthwise)

2 tbsp olive oil

2 tsp fresh rosemary (finely chopped)

Salt and pepper to taste

Instructions:

Preheat the oven to 400°F (200°C).

In a large mixing bowl, toss carrots with olive oil, rosemary, salt, and pepper.

Arrange the carrots on a baking sheet in a single layer.

Roast in the oven for about 20-25 minutes or until tender and slightly browned. Turn them occasionally to ensure even cooking. Serve warm.

Nutritional Data:
Calories: 120 | Carbohydrates: 11g | Protein: 1g | Fat: 8g | Fiber: 3g

Lemon Herb Asparagus

⭐⭐⭐⭐⭐ | Preparation Time: 10 mins | Cooking Time: 10 mins | Portion Size: 4

Ingredients:

400g asparagus (ends trimmed)

2 tbsp olive oil

Zest and juice of 1 lemon

1 tsp mixed herbs (such as basil, parsley, and thyme)

Salt and pepper to taste

Instructions:

In a large skillet, heat olive oil over medium heat.

Add asparagus and sauté for about 5-7 minutes until tender.

Stir in lemon zest, lemon juice, herbs, salt, and pepper.

Cook for an additional 2-3 minutes, ensuring the asparagus is well-coated. Serve hot.

Nutritional Data:
Calories: 90 | Carbohydrates: 5g | Protein: 3g | Fat: 7g | Fiber: 2g

Spiced Roasted Cauliflower

⭐⭐⭐⭐⭐ | Preparation Time: 10 mins | Cooking Time: 25 mins | Portion Size: 4

Ingredients:

1 large cauliflower (broken into florets)

2 tbsp olive oil

1 tsp ground cumin

1/2 tsp smoked paprika

Salt and pepper to taste

Instructions:

Preheat the oven to 425°F (220°C).

In a large mixing bowl, toss cauliflower florets with olive oil, cumin, smoked paprika, salt, and pepper.

Spread the cauliflower on a baking sheet in a single layer.

Roast in the oven for 20-25 minutes or until tender and edges are browned. Serve warm.

Nutritional Data:
Calories: 110 | Carbohydrates: 8g | Protein: 3g | Fat: 8g | Fiber: 3g

Minted Pea Purée

⭐⭐⭐⭐⭐ | Preparation Time: 10 mins | Cooking Time: 10 mins | Portion Size: 4

Ingredients:

2 cups green peas (frozen or fresh)

1/4 cup fresh mint leaves

2 tbsp olive oil

Salt and pepper to taste

Instructions:

In a pot of boiling water, cook the peas until they're just tender, about 5 minutes.

Drain the peas and transfer them to a blender or food processor.

Add mint leaves, olive oil, salt, and pepper. Blend until you achieve a smooth purée.

Adjust the seasoning if necessary and serve as a side or dip.

Nutritional Data:

Calories: 140 | Carbohydrates: 15g | Protein: 5g | Fat: 7g | Fiber: 5g

Fish and Seafood

Lemon-Dill Baked Salmon

⭐⭐⭐⭐⭐ | Preparation Time: 10 mins | Cooking Time: 20 mins | Portion Size: 4

Ingredients:

4 salmon fillets (around 150g each)

2 tbsp olive oil

Zest and juice of 1 lemon

2 tbsp fresh dill, chopped

Salt and pepper to taste

Instructions:

Preheat the oven to 375°F (190°C).

Place the salmon fillets in a baking dish.

In a bowl, mix together the olive oil, lemon zest, lemon juice, dill, salt, and pepper. Pour this mixture over the salmon.

Bake for 20 minutes or until salmon easily flakes with a fork.

Nutritional Data:

Calories: 280 | Carbohydrates: 1g | Protein: 25g | Fat: 20g | Fiber: 0g

Zesty Lime Shrimp Skewers

⭐⭐⭐⭐ | Preparation Time: 15 mins (plus marinating) | Cooking Time: 8 mins | Portion Size: 4

Ingredients:

500g large shrimp, peeled and deveined

Zest and juice of 2 limes

2 tbsp olive oil

1 tsp chili flakes (optional)

Salt to taste

Instructions:

In a bowl, combine lime zest, lime juice, olive oil, chili flakes, and salt. Mix well.

Add the shrimp to the bowl and toss to coat. Marinate for at least 30 minutes in the refrigerator.

Preheat the grill to medium heat.

Thread the shrimp onto skewers and grill for 3-4 minutes on each side or until pink and cooked through.

Nutritional Data:

Calories: 180 | Carbohydrates: 2g | Protein: 24g | Fat: 8g | Fiber: 0g

Tuna Nicoise Salad with Olive Dressing

⭐⭐⭐⭐ | Preparation Time: 20 mins | Cooking Time: 10 mins | Portion Size: 4

Ingredients:

4 fresh tuna steaks (around 150g each)

200g green beans, trimmed

4 hard-boiled eggs, quartered

2 cups cherry tomatoes, halved

1/4 cup black olives, pitted

2 tbsp capers

3 tbsp olive oil

1 tbsp red wine vinegar

Salt and pepper to taste

Instructions:

Boil the green beans in salted water for 5 minutes or until tender-crisp. Drain and rinse with cold water.

In a blender, combine olives, capers, olive oil, and red wine vinegar to make the dressing. Blend until smooth.

Season the tuna steaks with salt and pepper. Grill for 2-3 minutes on each side or until desired doneness.

Assemble the salad by placing green beans, tomatoes, and eggs on a plate. Top with the grilled tuna and drizzle with the olive dressing.

Nutritional Data:
Calories: 360 | Carbohydrates: 8g | Protein: 40g | Fat: 18g | Fiber: 3g

Garlic Herb Steamed Mussels

✯ ✯ ✯ ✯ ✯ | Preparation Time: 10 mins | Cooking Time: 10 mins | Portion Size: 4

Ingredients:

1kg mussels, cleaned

4 garlic cloves, minced

1/4 cup white wine

2 tbsp fresh parsley, chopped

1 tbsp olive oil

Salt and pepper to taste

Instructions:

In a large pot, heat the olive oil over medium heat. Add the garlic and sauté until fragrant.

Add the mussels to the pot along with the white wine, salt, and pepper.

Cover the pot and let the mussels steam for about 7-8 minutes or until they have opened up.

Discard any mussels that haven't opened. Sprinkle with fresh parsley before serving.

Nutritional Data:
Calories: 220 | Carbohydrates: 8g | Protein: 18g | Fat: 8g | Fiber: 0g

Quick Seafood Paella with Saffron

✯ ✯ ✯ ✯ ✯ | Preparation Time: 15 mins | Cooking Time: 30 mins | Portion Size: 4

Ingredients:

200g shrimp, peeled and deveined

200g mussels, cleaned

1 cup Arborio rice

1 onion, finely chopped

2 garlic cloves, minced

1/4 tsp saffron threads

3 cups chicken or vegetable broth, warm

2 tbsp olive oil

Salt and pepper to taste

Fresh parsley and lemon wedges for garnish

Instructions:

In a large skillet or paella pan, heat the olive oil. Add onions and garlic and sauté until translucent.

Add rice to the skillet and stir to coat with the oil.

Pour in the warm broth and sprinkle saffron threads. Stir well.

Allow the mixture to simmer for about 20 minutes, stirring occasionally.

Add the shrimp and mussels, ensuring they are nestled into the rice. Cook until the seafood is done and mussels have opened up.

Garnish with fresh parsley and serve with lemon wedges.

Nutritional Data:
Calories: 360 | Carbohydrates: 45g | Protein: 20g | Fat: 10g | Fiber: 1g

Seafood Pasta with Clams - Spaghetti alle Vongole

✯ ✯ ✯ ✯ ✯ | Preparation Time: 15 minutes | Cooking Time: 20 minutes | Serves: 4

Ingredients:

- 200g whole grain spaghetti
- 1kg fresh clams, cleaned and rinsed
- 3 tbsp extra virgin olive oil
- 4 cloves garlic, thinly sliced
- 1 small red chili, finely chopped (optional, for some heat)
- 1/2 cup low-sodium vegetable broth or white wine (for those watching alcohol intake, the broth is preferable)
- Freshly chopped parsley, for garnish

- Zest of 1 lemon
- Salt and pepper, to taste

Instructions:

1. **Pasta Preparation**: Boil a large pot of water with a pinch of salt. Once boiling, add the whole grain spaghetti and cook according to the package instructions until al dente. Drain the pasta, reserving about a cup of the pasta water, and set aside.
2. **Clam Preparation**: In a separate large pan, heat the olive oil over medium heat. Add the garlic slices and chili (if using) and sauté for about 1-2 minutes or until the garlic is lightly golden.
3. **Cooking Clams**: Add the clams to the pan and pour over the vegetable broth or white wine. Increase the heat to medium-high, cover with a lid, and let the clams cook for 5-7 minutes, or until they open up. Discard any clams that do not open.
4. **Combining Pasta and Clams**: Add the cooked spaghetti to the pan with clams. Toss everything gently, allowing the pasta to absorb some of the delicious flavors from the clam broth. If the mixture seems too dry, add a little reserved pasta water to achieve the desired consistency.
5. **Final Touch**: Season with salt (sparingly, as clams are naturally salty) and pepper. Add the freshly chopped parsley and lemon zest, giving everything a final toss.
6. **Serve**: Plate the spaghetti with clams in individual bowls, ensuring each portion gets an ample amount of clams and broth. Enjoy immediately.

Nutritional Data: Calories: 350kcal | Carbohydrates: 44g | Protein: 22g | Fats: 9g | Saturated Fat: 1.5g | Cholesterol: 50mg | Sodium: 180mg | Fiber: 5g | Sugars: 2g

Miso-Glazed Black Cod

☆ ☆ ☆ ☆ | Preparation Time: 10 mins (plus marinating) | Cooking Time: 15 mins | Portion Size: 4

Ingredients:

4 black cod fillets

3 tbsp white miso paste

2 tbsp mirin (rice wine)

1 tbsp soy sauce (low sodium)

1 tbsp honey

Instructions:

In a bowl, whisk together miso paste, mirin, soy sauce, and honey.

Coat the black cod fillets in the miso mixture and let them marinate for at least 2 hours, preferably overnight.

Preheat oven to 400°F (200°C).

Place marinated fillets on a baking sheet and bake for about 15 minutes or until fish flakes easily.

Serve with steamed rice or vegetables.

Nutritional Data:

Calories: 260 | Carbohydrates: 10g | Protein: 28g | Fat: 10g | Fiber: 0g

Easy Cilantro-Lime Tilapia

☆ ☆ ☆ ☆ | Preparation Time: 10 mins | Cooking Time: 10 mins | Portion Size: 4

Ingredients:

4 tilapia fillets

Juice of 2 limes

2 tbsp fresh cilantro, chopped

2 tbsp olive oil

Salt and pepper to taste

Instructions:

In a bowl, combine lime juice, cilantro, olive oil, salt, and pepper.

Marinate the tilapia fillets in this mixture for about 20 minutes.

Preheat a skillet over medium heat and add the marinated fillets.

Cook for about 4-5 minutes on each side or until the fish is cooked through.

Serve with a fresh salad or roasted veggies.

Nutritional Data:

Calories: 210 | Carbohydrates: 3g | Protein: 25g | Fat: 11g | Fiber: 0g

Shrimp and Broccoli Stir-Fry with Ginger

✿ ✿ ✿ ✿ ✿ | Preparation Time: 15 mins | Cooking Time: 10 mins | Portion Size: 4

Ingredients:

500g large shrimp, peeled and deveined

2 cups broccoli florets

1 red bell pepper, sliced

1 tbsp fresh ginger, minced

2 garlic cloves, minced

2 tbsp soy sauce (low sodium)

1 tbsp sesame oil

1 tsp honey

2 tbsp olive oil

Instructions:

In a small bowl, mix together soy sauce, sesame oil, and honey. Set aside.

Heat olive oil in a wok or large skillet. Add ginger and garlic and sauté for a minute.

Add the broccoli and bell pepper and stir-fry for about 3 minutes.

Add the shrimp and cook until they turn pink.

Pour the soy sauce mixture over the stir-fry and toss to coat well.

Serve with brown rice or quinoa.

Nutritional Data:

Calories: 240 | Carbohydrates: 10g | Protein: 28g | Fat: 10g | Fiber: 2g

Heart-Healthy Crab Cakes

✿ ✿ ✿ ✿ ✿ | Preparation Time: 20 mins | Cooking Time: 10 mins | Portion Size: 4

Ingredients:

450g lump crab meat

1/4 cup whole wheat breadcrumbs

1 egg, lightly beaten

2 tbsp Greek yogurt

1 tbsp Dijon mustard

1 tsp Old Bay seasoning

2 tbsp fresh parsley, chopped

2 tbsp olive oil

Instructions:

In a large bowl, combine crab meat, breadcrumbs, egg, Greek yogurt, Dijon mustard, Old Bay seasoning, and parsley. Mix well.

Form the mixture into small patties.

Heat olive oil in a skillet over medium heat. Add the crab cakes and cook for about 4-5 minutes on each side or until golden brown.

Serve with a lemon wedge or tartar sauce.

Nutritional Data:

Calories: 230 | Carbohydrates: 9g | Protein: 25g | Fat: 9g | Fiber: 1g

Zesty Lemon Salmon

✿ ✿ ✿ ✿ ✿ | Preparation Time: 15 mins | Cooking Time: 15 mins | Portion Size: 4

Ingredients:

4 salmon fillets

Zest and juice of 2 lemons

2 tbsp olive oil

2 garlic cloves, minced

Salt and pepper to taste

Fresh dill for garnish

Instructions:

In a bowl, mix together lemon zest, lemon juice, olive oil, garlic, salt, and pepper.

Marinate the salmon fillets in the mixture for at least 30 minutes.

Preheat oven to 400°F (200°C).

Place the marinated salmon fillets on a baking sheet.

Bake for about 15 minutes or until salmon easily flakes with a fork.

Garnish with fresh dill and serve.

Nutritional Data:
Calories: 280 | Carbohydrates: 2g | Protein: 30g | Fat: 16g | Fiber: 0g

Mediterranean Mussels with White Wine

⭐ ⭐ ⭐ ⭐ ⭐ | Preparation Time: 10 mins | Cooking Time: 10 mins | Portion Size: 4

Ingredients:
1 kg mussels, cleaned and debearded
1 cup dry white wine
1 onion, chopped
3 garlic cloves, minced
2 tbsp olive oil
Fresh parsley, chopped
Salt and pepper to taste

Instructions:
In a large pot, heat the olive oil. Add onions and garlic and sauté until translucent.

Pour in the white wine and bring to a simmer.

Add mussels to the pot. Cover and let them cook for about 7-8 minutes or until they open up.

Discard any mussels that don't open.

Season with salt, pepper, and garnish with fresh parsley.

Serve with crusty whole grain bread.

Nutritional Data:
Calories: 210 | Carbohydrates: 8g | Protein: 20g | Fat: 8g | Fiber: 1g

Sesame Seared Ahi Tuna

⭐ ⭐ ⭐ ⭐ ⭐ | Preparation Time: 15 mins | Cooking Time: 4 mins | Portion Size: 4

Ingredients:
4 ahi tuna steaks
1/4 cup black and white sesame seeds
2 tbsp soy sauce (low sodium)
1 tbsp sesame oil
Wasabi and pickled ginger for serving

Instructions:
Mix the soy sauce and sesame oil in a bowl. Marinate the tuna steaks for about 10 minutes.

Spread the sesame seeds on a plate.

Remove the tuna from the marinade and press each side into the sesame seeds.

Heat a skillet over high heat. Once hot, add the tuna steaks and sear for about 1-2 minutes on each side. The outside should be golden and the inside should remain pink.

Slice and serve with wasabi and pickled ginger.

Nutritional Data:
Calories: 250 | Carbohydrates: 5g | Protein: 30g | Fat: 11g | Fiber: 1g

Garlic Lemon Butter Shrimp

⭐ ⭐ ⭐ ⭐ ⭐ | Preparation Time: 10 mins | Cooking Time: 10 mins | Portion Size: 4

Ingredients:
500g large shrimp, peeled and deveined
4 tbsp olive oil
4 garlic cloves, minced
Zest and juice of 1 lemon
Salt and pepper to taste
2 tbsp fresh parsley, chopped

Instructions:
In a skillet, heat olive oil over medium heat. Add the minced garlic and sauté until fragrant.

Add the shrimp to the skillet and cook until pink, about 3-4 minutes per side.

Stir in lemon zest, lemon juice, and season with salt and pepper.

Garnish with fresh parsley and serve immediately.

Nutritional Data:

Calories: 200 | Carbohydrates: 3g | Protein: 25g | Fat: 9g | Fiber: 0g

Chili Lime Cod Fillets

⋆ ⋆ ⋆ ⋆ ⋆ | Preparation Time: 15 mins | Cooking Time: 12 mins | Portion Size: 4

Ingredients:

4 cod fillets

2 tbsp olive oil

Zest and juice of 2 limes

1 tsp chili powder

1/4 tsp cumin

Salt and pepper to taste

Fresh cilantro for garnish

Instructions:

Preheat oven to 400°F (200°C).

In a bowl, mix together olive oil, lime zest, lime juice, chili powder, cumin, salt, and pepper.

Place cod fillets on a baking sheet and brush with the chili lime mixture.

Bake for about 10-12 minutes or until fish easily flakes with a fork.

Garnish with fresh cilantro and serve.

Nutritional Data:

Calories: 190 | Carbohydrates: 2g | Protein: 25g | Fat: 9g | Fiber: 1g

Heart-Healthy Seafood Paella

⋆ ⋆ ⋆ ⋆ ⋆ | Preparation Time: 25 mins | Cooking Time: 35 mins | Portion Size: 6

Ingredients:

1 cup whole grain rice

200g shrimp, peeled and deveined

200g mussels, cleaned and debearded

200g clams, cleaned

200g squid, sliced into rings

1 onion, diced

1 bell pepper, sliced

2 tomatoes, diced

3 garlic cloves, minced

1/4 tsp saffron threads

2 tbsp olive oil

Salt and pepper to taste

Fresh parsley and lemon wedges for garnish

Instructions:

In a large pan, heat olive oil over medium heat. Add onions, bell pepper, and garlic and sauté until soft.

Stir in tomatoes and cook for another 5 minutes.

Add rice to the pan and stir to coat with the vegetables.

Pour in 2 cups of water and add saffron threads, salt, and pepper. Cover and let it simmer for about 20 minutes.

Add shrimp, mussels, clams, and squid. Cover and cook for another 10-15 minutes or until seafood is cooked and rice is tender.

Garnish with fresh parsley and serve with lemon wedges.

Nutritional Data:

Calories: 320 | Carbohydrates: 40g | Protein: 25g | Fat: 7g | Fiber: 3g

Paprika-Spiced Tilapia

⋆ ⋆ ⋆ ⋆ ⋆ | Preparation Time: 15 mins | Cooking Time: 10 mins | Portion Size: 4

Ingredients:

4 tilapia fillets

2 tbsp olive oil

2 tsp paprika

1 tsp garlic powder

Salt and pepper to taste

Lemon wedges for serving

Instructions:

Mix paprika, garlic powder, salt, and pepper in a bowl.

Rub the spice mixture onto both sides of the tilapia fillets.

Heat olive oil in a skillet over medium heat. Once hot, add the tilapia and cook for about 4-5 minutes on each side or until golden and flaky.

Serve with lemon wedges.

Nutritional Data:

Calories: 210 | Carbohydrates: 1g | Protein: 28g | Fat: 9g | Fiber: 0g

Simple Poached Salmon with Dill Sauce

⭐ ⭐ ⭐ ⭐ ⭐ | Preparation Time: 10 mins | Cooking Time: 15 mins | Portion Size: 4

Ingredients:

4 salmon fillets

2 cups water

1 cup white wine

1 lemon, sliced

1/4 cup Greek yogurt

2 tbsp fresh dill, chopped

Salt and pepper to taste

Instructions:

In a large skillet, combine water, white wine, and lemon slices. Bring to a gentle simmer.

Season salmon with salt and pepper and add them to the skillet. Poach for about 10-12 minutes or until salmon is cooked through.

In a separate bowl, combine Greek yogurt and dill. Season with salt and pepper.

Serve salmon with a dollop of dill sauce.

Nutritional Data:

Calories: 280 | Carbohydrates: 4g | Protein: 30g | Fat: 10g | Fiber: 0g

Grilled Swordfish with Olive Tapenade

⭐ ⭐ ⭐ ⭐ ⭐ | Preparation Time: 20 mins | Cooking Time: 10 mins | Portion Size: 4

Ingredients:

4 swordfish steaks

1 cup pitted black olives

2 garlic cloves

2 tbsp capers

Zest and juice of 1 lemon

3 tbsp olive oil

Fresh parsley, chopped

Instructions:

For the tapenade, in a food processor, combine olives, garlic, capers, lemon zest, lemon juice, and 2 tbsp olive oil. Pulse until finely chopped.

Preheat the grill to medium-high heat. Brush swordfish steaks with the remaining olive oil and season with salt and pepper.

Grill swordfish for about 5 minutes on each side or until cooked through.

Serve with a spoonful of olive tapenade and garnish with chopped parsley.

Nutritional Data:

Calories: 320 | Carbohydrates: 3g | Protein: 35g | Fat: 18g | Fiber: 1g

Baked Haddock with Tomato and Basil

⭐ ⭐ ⭐ ⭐ ⭐ | Preparation Time: 10 mins | Cooking Time: 20 mins | Portion Size: 4

Ingredients:

4 haddock fillets

2 tomatoes, sliced

1/4 cup fresh basil, chopped

2 garlic cloves, minced

2 tbsp olive oil

Salt and pepper to taste

Instructions:

Preheat oven to 375°F (190°C).

In a baking dish, place haddock fillets. Drizzle with olive oil and season with salt, pepper, and minced garlic.

Top each fillet with tomato slices and chopped basil.

Bake for about 20 minutes or until fish flakes easily with a fork.

Serve immediately.

Nutritional Data:

Calories: 210 | Carbohydrates: 4g | Protein: 30g | Fat: 8g | Fiber: 1g

Shrimp and Avocado Salad

⭐⭐⭐⭐ | Preparation Time: 15 mins | Cooking Time: 5 mins | Portion Size: 4

Ingredients:

500g shrimp, peeled and deveined

2 avocados, diced

1 red bell pepper, diced

1/4 cup red onion, finely chopped

Juice of 2 limes

2 tbsp olive oil

Salt and pepper to taste

Fresh cilantro, chopped

Instructions:

In a skillet, heat 1 tbsp olive oil. Add shrimp and cook until pink, about 2-3 minutes on each side. Remove from heat and let cool.

In a large bowl, combine shrimp, avocado, red bell pepper, and red onion.

Drizzle with lime juice and the remaining olive oil. Season with salt, pepper, and toss to combine.

Garnish with chopped cilantro and serve.

Nutritional Data:

Calories: 290 | Carbohydrates: 12g | Protein: 25g | Fat: 17g | Fiber: 7g

Mango Salsa Mahi-Mahi

⭐⭐⭐⭐ | Preparation Time: 20 mins | Cooking Time: 12 mins | Portion Size: 4

Ingredients:

4 mahi-mahi fillets

1 ripe mango, diced

1/4 cup red bell pepper, diced

1/4 cup red onion, diced

1 jalapeño, minced (seeds removed)

Juice of 1 lime

2 tbsp fresh cilantro, chopped

2 tbsp olive oil

Salt and pepper to taste

Instructions:

In a bowl, combine mango, red bell pepper, red onion, jalapeño, lime juice, and cilantro. Mix well and season with salt. Set aside.

Season mahi-mahi fillets with salt and pepper. Heat olive oil in a skillet over medium heat. Cook fillets for about 5-6 minutes on each side or until golden brown and cooked through.

Serve mahi-mahi topped with mango salsa.

Nutritional Data:

Calories: 260 | Carbohydrates: 15g | Protein: 30g | Fat: 9g | Fiber: 2g

Grilled Sardines with Lemon and Rosemary

⭐⭐⭐⭐⭐ | Preparation Time: 10 mins | Cooking Time: 6 mins | Portion Size: 4

Ingredients:

8 fresh sardines, cleaned and gutted

2 lemons, 1 sliced and 1 for juice

4 sprigs fresh rosemary

2 tbsp olive oil

Salt and pepper to taste

Instructions:

Preheat grill to medium-high heat.

Season sardines with salt, pepper, and drizzle with olive oil. Insert a slice of lemon and a sprig of rosemary into each sardine.

Grill sardines for about 3 minutes on each side or until cooked through.

Drizzle with fresh lemon juice and serve immediately.

Nutritional Data:

Calories: 200 | Carbohydrates: 5g | Protein: 20g | Fat: 12g | Fiber: 1g

Tuna Steak with Pepper and Avocado Cucumber Salsa

⭐⭐ Preparation Time: 15 minutes | Cooking Time: 10 minutes | Portion Size: 4 servings

Ingredients:

- 4 fresh tuna steaks (about 6 oz each)
- 1 tablespoon extra-virgin olive oil
- Salt and freshly ground black pepper, to taste
- 1 ripe avocado, diced
- 1 cucumber, diced
- 1 red bell pepper, diced
- 1/4 cup fresh cilantro, chopped
- 1 lime, juiced
- 1 small red chili, finely chopped (optional for some heat)
- 2 green onions, thinly sliced

Instructions:

1. Preheat the grill or a grill pan to medium-high heat.
2. Rub the tuna steaks with olive oil, then season with salt and pepper.
3. Place the tuna steaks on the grill and cook for about 3-4 minutes on each side for medium-rare, or longer if desired.
4. While the tuna is cooking, prepare the salsa: In a large bowl, combine the avocado, cucumber, bell pepper, cilantro, lime juice, chili (if using), and green onions. Toss gently to mix. Season with salt and pepper to taste.
5. Once the tuna steaks are done, remove them from the grill and let them rest for a couple of minutes.
6. Serve the grilled tuna steaks with a generous spoonful of the avocado cucumber salsa on top.

Nutritional Data:

Calories: 320 | Total Fat: 14g | Saturated Fat: 2.5g | Cholesterol: 60mg | Sodium: 60mg | Total Carbohydrates: 10g | Dietary Fiber: 5g | Sugars: 3g | Protein: 35g

Herbed Tuna Steaks with Olive Relish

⭐⭐⭐⭐⭐ | Preparation Time: 20 mins | Cooking Time: 8 mins | Portion Size: 4

Ingredients:

4 tuna steaks

1/2 cup pitted green olives, chopped

1/4 cup fresh parsley, chopped

2 tbsp capers

1 lemon, zest and juice

3 tbsp olive oil

1 tsp dried oregano

Salt and pepper to taste

Instructions:

In a bowl, combine olives, parsley, capers, lemon zest, lemon juice, and 2 tbsp olive oil. Mix well and set aside.

Season tuna steaks with salt, pepper, oregano, and drizzle with the remaining olive oil.

Preheat a grill or grill pan to medium-high heat. Cook tuna steaks for about 3-4 minutes on each side or until desired doneness.
Serve tuna steaks topped with olive relish.

Nutritional Data:
Calories: 290 | Carbohydrates: 5g | Protein: 30g | Fat: 16g | Fiber: 1g

Zesty Lime and Garlic Shrimp Tacos

⭐⭐⭐⭐ | Preparation Time: 15 mins | Cooking Time: 8 mins | Portion Size: 4

Ingredients:
500g shrimp, peeled and deveined
Zest and juice of 2 limes
3 garlic cloves, minced
1 tsp chili powder
8 small whole wheat tortillas
1 cup lettuce, shredded
1/2 cup low-fat yogurt
2 tbsp olive oil
Salt and pepper to taste

Instructions:
In a bowl, mix lime zest, lime juice, garlic, chili powder, salt, and pepper. Add shrimp and marinate for about 10 minutes.
In a skillet, heat olive oil over medium heat. Cook shrimp for about 3-4 minutes on each side or until they turn pink.
Warm tortillas according to package instructions.
Assemble tacos by placing lettuce on a tortilla, followed by shrimp, and a dollop of yogurt.
Serve immediately.

Nutritional Data:
Calories: 320 | Carbohydrates: 25g | Protein: 28g | Fat: 12g | Fiber: 4g

Herb-Crusted Cod with Asparagus

⭐⭐⭐⭐⭐ | Preparation Time: 15 mins | Cooking Time: 15 mins | Portion Size: 4

Ingredients:
4 cod fillets
1 bunch asparagus, trimmed
1/4 cup breadcrumbs
2 tbsp fresh parsley, chopped
1 tbsp fresh dill, chopped
2 tbsp olive oil
Salt and pepper to taste

Instructions:
Preheat oven to 400°F (200°C).
In a bowl, mix breadcrumbs, parsley, dill, salt, and pepper.
Drizzle olive oil over cod fillets and then coat with the herb-breadcrumb mixture.
Place cod and asparagus on a baking sheet. Drizzle asparagus with a bit of olive oil and season with salt and pepper.
Bake for about 15 minutes or until cod is flaky and asparagus is tender.
Serve immediately.

Nutritional Data:
Calories: 210 | Carbohydrates: 10g | Protein: 25g | Fat: 8g | Fiber: 3g

Spicy Grilled Tilapia with Mango Salsa

⭐⭐⭐⭐⭐ | Preparation Time: 20 mins | Cooking Time: 10 mins | Portion Size: 4

Ingredients:
4 tilapia fillets
1 mango, diced
1/4 cup red bell pepper, diced
1/4 cup red onion, diced
1 jalapeño, minced
Juice of 1 lime
2 tbsp fresh cilantro, chopped

2 tbsp olive oil

1 tsp cayenne pepper

Salt and pepper to taste

Instructions:

In a bowl, combine mango, red bell pepper, red onion, jalapeño, lime juice, and cilantro. Season with salt and set aside.

Drizzle tilapia with olive oil and season with cayenne pepper, salt, and black pepper.

Preheat a grill or grill pan to medium-high heat. Cook tilapia for about 4-5 minutes on each side or until cooked through.

Serve tilapia topped with mango salsa.

Nutritional Data:

Calories: 230 | Carbohydrates: 15g | Protein: 28g | Fat: 8g | Fiber: 2g

Chili Lemon Crab Cakes

⭐ ⭐ ⭐ ⭐ | Preparation Time: 20 mins | Cooking Time: 10 mins | Portion Size: 4

Ingredients:

500g crabmeat

1/2 cup breadcrumbs

Zest and juice of 1 lemon

1 egg, beaten

2 green onions, chopped

1 tsp chili powder

2 tbsp olive oil

Salt and pepper to taste

Instructions:

In a bowl, combine crabmeat, breadcrumbs, lemon zest, lemon juice, egg, green onions, chili powder, salt, and pepper. Mix until well combined.

Form into 8 patties.

Heat olive oil in a skillet over medium heat. Cook crab cakes for about 4-5 minutes on each side or until golden brown.

Serve with a lemon wedge.

Nutritional Data:

Calories: 240 | Carbohydrates: 10g | Protein: 25g | Fat: 10g | Fiber: 1g

Ginger Soy Salmon Bowl

⭐ ⭐ ⭐ ⭐ ⭐ | Preparation Time: 20 mins | Cooking Time: 15 mins | Portion Size: 4

Ingredients:

4 salmon fillets

2 cups brown rice, cooked

1/4 cup low-sodium soy sauce

2 tbsp fresh ginger, grated

2 garlic cloves, minced

2 green onions, sliced

1 cup broccoli florets, steamed

1 tbsp sesame seeds

2 tbsp olive oil

Salt and pepper to taste

Instructions:

In a bowl, mix soy sauce, ginger, and garlic.

Place salmon fillets in the marinade and let them sit for 10 minutes.

Heat olive oil in a skillet over medium heat. Cook salmon for about 4-5 minutes on each side or until flaky.

In serving bowls, place a scoop of brown rice, top with salmon, steamed broccoli, green onions, and sesame seeds.

Drizzle remaining marinade sauce over the top and serve.

Nutritional Data:

Calories: 370 | Carbohydrates: 45g | Protein: 32g | Fat: 8g | Fiber: 4g

Lemon Herb Prawns and Zoodles

⭐ ⭐ ⭐ ⭐ ⭐ | Preparation Time: 20 mins | Cooking Time: 10 mins | Portion Size: 4

Ingredients:

500g prawns, peeled and deveined

4 zucchinis, spiralized

Zest and juice of 2 lemons

2 tbsp fresh parsley, chopped

1 tbsp fresh dill, chopped

2 tbsp olive oil

Salt and pepper to taste

Instructions:

In a bowl, mix lemon zest, lemon juice, parsley, dill, salt, and pepper.

Add prawns to the marinade and let them sit for 10 minutes.

Heat 1 tbsp olive oil in a skillet over medium heat. Cook prawns for about 2-3 minutes on each side or until pink.

In another skillet, heat 1 tbsp olive oil. Sauté spiralized zucchini for 3-4 minutes or until al dente.

Serve prawns over zoodles and garnish with additional herbs if desired.

Nutritional Data:

Calories: 250 | Carbohydrates: 12g | Protein: 28g | Fat: 10g | Fiber: 3g

---

Cilantro Lime Tuna Salad

✿ ✿ ✿ ✿ ✿ | Preparation Time: 20 mins | Cooking Time: 0 mins | Portion Size: 4

Ingredients:

2 cans of tuna, drained

1/4 cup cilantro, finely chopped

Zest and juice of 2 limes

1/4 cup red bell pepper, diced

2 tbsp low-fat mayonnaise

Salt and pepper to taste

Instructions:

In a bowl, combine tuna, cilantro, lime zest, lime juice, red bell pepper, and mayonnaise. Mix until well combined.

Season with salt and pepper to taste.

Serve on whole-grain bread or as a salad topping.

Nutritional Data:

Calories: 150 | Carbohydrates: 3g | Protein: 25g | Fat: 4g | Fiber: 1g

---

Garlic Butter Scallops with Spinach

✿ ✿ ✿ ✿ ✿ | Preparation Time: 10 mins | Cooking Time: 10 mins | Portion Size: 4

Ingredients:

500g scallops

4 cups fresh spinach

4 garlic cloves, minced

2 tbsp unsalted butter

2 tbsp olive oil

Salt and pepper to taste

Instructions:

Heat 1 tbsp olive oil in a skillet over medium heat. Add garlic and sauté for a minute.

Add scallops and cook for about 2-3 minutes on each side or until golden.

Remove scallops and set them aside.

In the same skillet, add butter and remaining olive oil. Add spinach and sauté until wilted.

Serve scallops over a bed of spinach.

Nutritional Data:

Calories: 210 | Carbohydrates: 4g | Protein: 21g | Fat: 12g | Fiber: 1g

Meat

Herb-Crusted Grilled Chicken Salad

☆☆☆☆☆ | Preparation Time: 15 mins | Cooking Time: 20 mins | Portion Size: 4

Ingredients:

4 boneless, skinless chicken breasts

2 tbsp olive oil

2 tsp rosemary, finely chopped

2 tsp thyme, finely chopped

Salt and pepper to taste

6 cups mixed salad greens

1 cup cherry tomatoes, halved

1/2 cucumber, sliced

Instructions:

Preheat grill to medium heat.

Rub chicken breasts with olive oil, rosemary, thyme, salt, and pepper.

Grill chicken for 10 minutes on each side or until fully cooked.

Slice chicken and serve over mixed greens, cherry tomatoes, and cucumber.

Nutritional Data:

Calories: 260 | Carbohydrates: 6g | Protein: 28g | Fat: 14g | Fiber: 2g

Lemon-Thyme Turkey Skewers

☆☆☆☆☆ | Preparation Time: 25 mins (incl. marination) | Cooking Time: 15 mins | Portion Size: 4

Ingredients:

500g turkey breast, cubed

Zest and juice of 2 lemons

2 tsp thyme, finely chopped

2 tbsp olive oil

Salt and pepper to taste

Wooden skewers, soaked in water

Instructions:

In a bowl, combine lemon zest, lemon juice, thyme, olive oil, salt, and pepper. Add turkey cubes and marinate for 20 minutes.

Preheat grill to medium heat.

Thread turkey cubes onto skewers.

Grill skewers for 7-8 minutes on each side or until turkey is fully cooked.

Nutritional Data:

Calories: 220 | Carbohydrates: 3g | Protein: 32g | Fat: 9g | Fiber: 1g

Rosemary Garlic Pork Tenderloin

☆☆☆☆☆ | Preparation Time: 10 mins | Cooking Time: 25 mins | Portion Size: 4

Ingredients:

1 pork tenderloin (about 500g)

3 garlic cloves, minced

2 tsp rosemary, finely chopped

2 tbsp olive oil

Salt and pepper to taste

Instructions:

Preheat oven to 190°C (375°F).

Rub pork tenderloin with garlic, rosemary, olive oil, salt, and pepper.

Place in a roasting pan and bake for 25 minutes or until fully cooked.

Allow to rest for 5 minutes before slicing and serving.

Nutritional Data:

Calories: 240 | Carbohydrates: 2g | Protein: 32g | Fat: 11g | Fiber: 0.5g

Honey-Mustard Grilled Chicken Breasts

✩ ✩ ✩ ✩ | Preparation Time: 15 mins | Cooking Time: 15 mins | Portion Size: 4

Ingredients:

4 boneless, skinless chicken breasts

2 tbsp honey

2 tbsp Dijon mustard

1 tbsp olive oil

Salt and pepper to taste

Instructions:

In a bowl, mix honey, Dijon mustard, olive oil, salt, and pepper.

Brush mixture over chicken breasts.

Preheat grill to medium heat and cook chicken for 7 minutes on each side or until fully cooked.

Serve hot.

Nutritional Data:

Calories: 220 | Carbohydrates: 9g | Protein: 27g | Fat: 7g | Fiber: 0g

Spiced Lamb Chops with Mint Yogurt

✩ ✩ ✩ ✩ | Preparation Time: 20 mins | Cooking Time: 10 mins | Portion Size: 4

Ingredients:

8 lean lamb chops

1 tsp cumin

1 tsp paprika

Salt and pepper to taste

1 cup low-fat yogurt

2 tbsp fresh mint, finely chopped

Instructions:

Rub lamb chops with cumin, paprika, salt, and pepper.

Grill lamb chops for 5 minutes on each side.

Mix yogurt and mint to make the sauce.

Serve lamb chops hot with mint yogurt on the side.

Nutritional Data:

Calories: 260 | Carbohydrates: 6g | Protein: 30g | Fat: 12g | Fiber: 1g

Balsamic Glazed Turkey Meatballs

✩ ✩ ✩ ✩ ✩ | Preparation Time: 15 mins | Cooking Time: 20 mins | Portion Size: 4

Ingredients:

500g lean ground turkey

1/2 cup oats

1 egg, beaten

2 garlic cloves, minced

1/2 cup balsamic vinegar

2 tbsp olive oil

Salt and pepper to taste

Instructions:

In a bowl, mix turkey, oats, egg, garlic, salt, and pepper. Form into meatballs.

Heat olive oil in a pan and cook meatballs for 10-12 minutes.

Add balsamic vinegar and simmer until the sauce thickens.

Serve meatballs hot, drizzled with balsamic glaze.

Nutritional Data:

Calories: 290 | Carbohydrates: 14g | Protein: 28g | Fat: 13g | Fiber: 2g

Herb-Stuffed Roast Chicken

✩ ✩ ✩ ✩ | Preparation Time: 20 mins | Cooking Time: 1 hr 20 mins | Portion Size: 4

Ingredients:

1 whole chicken (about 1.5kg)

2 tbsp olive oil

3 garlic cloves, minced

1 lemon, zest and juice

2 tsp rosemary, finely chopped

2 tsp thyme, finely chopped

Salt and pepper to taste

Instructions:

Preheat oven to 190°C (375°F).

Mix garlic, lemon zest, lemon juice, rosemary, thyme, olive oil, salt, and pepper in a bowl.

Rub the mixture all over the chicken, inside and out.

Place chicken in a roasting pan, breast side up, and roast for 1 hour and 20 minutes or until cooked through.

Let it rest for 10 minutes before serving.

Nutritional Data:

Calories: 320 | Carbohydrates: 5g | Protein: 40g | Fat: 16g | Fiber: 1g

Ginger-Sesame Beef Stir-Fry

☆ ☆ ☆ ☆ ☆ | Preparation Time: 15 mins | Cooking Time: 20 mins | Portion Size: 4

Ingredients:

500g lean beef strips

1 tbsp ginger, minced

2 garlic cloves, minced

2 tbsp sesame oil

2 tbsp low-sodium soy sauce

1 bell pepper, sliced

1 onion, sliced

1 carrot, julienned

2 tbsp toasted sesame seeds

Instructions:

Heat 1 tbsp sesame oil in a wok or large pan over medium heat. Add beef strips and stir-fry until browned. Remove and set aside.

In the same pan, add another tbsp of sesame oil, ginger, and garlic. Sauté for 1 minute.

Add bell pepper, onion, and carrot. Stir-fry for 5-6 minutes.

Add beef back to the pan, pour soy sauce, and cook for another 3 minutes.

Garnish with toasted sesame seeds and serve hot.

Nutritional Data:

Calories: 280 | Carbohydrates: 9g | Protein: 32g | Fat: 13g | Fiber: 2g

Olive and Tomato Braised Lamb Shanks

☆ ☆ ☆ ☆ | Preparation Time: 10 mins | Cooking Time: 2 hrs | Portion Size: 4

Ingredients:

4 lamb shanks

1 can (400g) diced tomatoes

1/2 cup olives, pitted

2 onions, sliced

3 garlic cloves, minced

2 tbsp olive oil

Salt and pepper to taste

1 cup chicken broth (low sodium)

Instructions:

Preheat oven to 150°C (300°F).

In a large oven-proof pot, heat olive oil over medium heat. Brown lamb shanks and set aside.

In the same pot, sauté onions and garlic until translucent.

Return lamb shanks to the pot. Add diced tomatoes, olives, chicken broth, salt, and pepper.

Cover and transfer to the oven. Cook for 2 hours or until lamb is tender.

Serve hot, garnished with additional olives if desired.

Nutritional Data:

Calories: 350 | Carbohydrates: 10g | Protein: 35g | Fat: 18g | Fiber: 2g

Rosemary and Garlic Grilled Steak

⭐⭐⭐⭐⭐ | Preparation Time: 15 mins | Cooking Time: 12 mins | Portion Size: 4

Ingredients:

4 lean beef steaks

2 tbsp fresh rosemary, finely chopped

3 garlic cloves, minced

2 tbsp olive oil

Salt and pepper to taste

Instructions:

Mix rosemary, garlic, olive oil, salt, and pepper in a bowl.

Rub the mixture over the steaks, ensuring they are well-coated.

Preheat the grill to high. Grill the steaks for about 5-6 minutes each side or until desired doneness.

Let rest for 5 minutes before serving.

Nutritional Data:

Calories: 330 | Carbohydrates: 1g | Protein: 34g | Fat: 20g | Fiber: 0g

Paprika Pork Tenderloin

⭐⭐⭐⭐ | Preparation Time: 10 mins | Cooking Time: 25 mins | Portion Size: 4

Ingredients:

2 pork tenderloins (about 500g each)

2 tsp smoked paprika

1 tsp garlic powder

1 tbsp olive oil

Salt and pepper to taste

Instructions:

Preheat oven to 190°C (375°F).

Combine paprika, garlic powder, olive oil, salt, and pepper in a bowl.

Rub the mixture over the pork tenderloins.

Place tenderloins in a roasting pan and roast for 25 minutes or until cooked through.

Let rest for 5 minutes before slicing and serving.

Nutritional Data:

Calories: 280 | Carbohydrates: 1g | Protein: 40g | Fat: 11g | Fiber: 0g

Basil and Lemon Chicken Skewers

⭐⭐⭐⭐ | Preparation Time: 20 mins (plus marinating time) | Cooking Time: 10 mins | Portion Size: 4

Ingredients:

500g chicken breast, cubed

Zest and juice of 1 lemon

2 tbsp fresh basil, finely chopped

2 tbsp olive oil

Salt and pepper to taste

Instructions:

Mix lemon zest, lemon juice, basil, olive oil, salt, and pepper in a bowl.

Add chicken cubes to the marinade and ensure they are well-coated. Marinate for at least 1 hour.

Thread the chicken cubes onto skewers.

Preheat the grill to medium-high heat. Grill skewers for 5 minutes on each side or until chicken is cooked through.

Serve hot with a side of your choice.

Nutritional Data:

Calories: 230 | Carbohydrates: 2g | Protein: 30g | Fat: 10g | Fiber: 0g

Honey Mustard Glazed Pork Chops

⭐⭐⭐⭐ | Preparation Time: 10 mins | Cooking Time: 20 mins | Portion Size: 4

Ingredients:

4 boneless pork chops

2 tbsp honey

2 tbsp Dijon mustard

1 tbsp olive oil

Salt and pepper to taste

1 tsp chopped fresh thyme

Instructions:

In a bowl, mix honey, Dijon mustard, thyme, salt, and pepper.

Coat each pork chop with the honey mustard mixture.

In a skillet, heat olive oil over medium-high heat. Add pork chops and cook for about 7 minutes each side or until golden brown and cooked through.

Serve hot with a side of steamed vegetables.

Nutritional Data:

Calories: 280 | Carbohydrates: 9g | Protein: 31g | Fat: 13g | Fiber: 0g

Spiced Lamb Meatballs with Tomato Sauce

⭐⭐⭐⭐⭐ | Preparation Time: 20 mins | Cooking Time: 30 mins | Portion Size: 4

Ingredients:

500g ground lamb

1 onion, finely chopped

2 garlic cloves, minced

1 tsp ground cumin

1 tsp ground coriander

400g canned tomatoes

1 tbsp olive oil

Salt and pepper to taste

Fresh parsley for garnish

Instructions:

Mix ground lamb, half of the onion, half of the garlic, cumin, coriander, salt, and pepper in a bowl. Form into small meatballs.

Heat olive oil in a skillet over medium heat. Brown the meatballs on all sides and set aside.

In the same skillet, add the remaining onion and garlic and sauté until translucent. Add canned tomatoes and bring to a simmer.

Return meatballs to the skillet and let them simmer in the tomato sauce for 20 minutes.

Garnish with fresh parsley before serving.

Nutritional Data:

Calories: 340 | Carbohydrates: 10g | Protein: 20g | Fat: 24g | Fiber: 2g

Beef and Broccoli Stir-Fry

⭐⭐⭐⭐⭐ | Preparation Time: 15 mins | Cooking Time: 15 mins | Portion Size: 4

Ingredients:

500g lean beef strips

2 cups broccoli florets

2 garlic cloves, minced

2 tbsp low-sodium soy sauce

1 tbsp olive oil

1 tbsp sesame oil

1 tsp ground ginger

Instructions:

Heat olive oil in a wok or large pan over medium-high heat. Add beef strips and stir-fry until browned. Remove and set aside.

In the same pan, add sesame oil, garlic, and ginger. Sauté for 1 minute.

Add broccoli florets and stir-fry for 5 minutes.

Return beef to the pan, pour in soy sauce, and stir well. Cook for another 2-3 minutes.

Serve hot with brown rice or quinoa.

Nutritional Data:

Calories: 290 | Carbohydrates: 8g | Protein: 30g | Fat: 15g | Fiber: 2g

Mediterranean Stuffed Chicken Breasts

☆ ☆ ☆ ☆ ☆ | Preparation Time: 20 mins | Cooking Time: 25 mins | Portion Size: 4

Ingredients:

4 boneless, skinless chicken breasts

1/2 cup feta cheese, crumbled

1/4 cup sun-dried tomatoes, chopped

2 tbsp fresh basil, chopped

1 tbsp olive oil

Salt and pepper to taste

Instructions:

Preheat oven to 200°C (390°F).

Make a pocket in each chicken breast by slicing horizontally through the center, being careful not to cut all the way through.

Mix feta cheese, sun-dried tomatoes, and basil in a bowl.

Stuff each chicken breast pocket with the feta mixture.

Season chicken breasts with salt and pepper and drizzle with olive oil.

Place chicken breasts in a baking dish and bake for 20-25 minutes or until chicken is cooked through.

Serve hot with a salad or steamed veggies.

Nutritional Data:

Calories: 270 | Carbohydrates: 6g | Protein: 28g | Fat: 14g | Fiber: 1g

Herb-Crusted Lamb Chops

☆ ☆ ☆ ☆ ☆ | Preparation Time: 15 mins | Cooking Time: 20 mins | Portion Size: 4

Ingredients:

8 lamb chops

2 tbsp fresh rosemary, chopped

2 tbsp fresh thyme, chopped

2 garlic cloves, minced

1 tbsp olive oil

Salt and pepper to taste

Instructions:

Mix rosemary, thyme, garlic, olive oil, salt, and pepper in a bowl.

Rub the herb mixture on both sides of each lamb chop.

Heat a grill pan or skillet over medium-high heat. Cook lamb chops for about 3-4 minutes on each side or until desired doneness.

Serve with roasted vegetables or a fresh salad.

Nutritional Data:

Calories: 320 | Carbohydrates: 2g | Protein: 25g | Fat: 23g | Fiber: 0g

Tenderloin Tips with Mushroom and Onion Gravy

☆ ☆ ☆ ☆ ☆ | Preparation Time: 20 mins | Cooking Time: 30 mins | Portion Size: 4

Ingredients:

500g beef tenderloin tips

1 cup mushrooms, sliced

1 onion, sliced

2 cups beef broth (low-sodium)

1 tbsp olive oil

1 tbsp whole wheat flour

Salt and pepper to taste

Instructions:

In a skillet, heat olive oil over medium-high heat. Add tenderloin tips and sear until browned on all sides. Remove and set aside.

In the same skillet, add mushrooms and onions. Cook until softened.

Sprinkle flour over the mushroom-onion mixture and stir well.

Gradually add beef broth, stirring continuously to avoid lumps. Let it simmer until the gravy thickens.

Return the beef tips to the skillet and let them simmer in the gravy for 10 minutes.

Season with salt and pepper and serve hot with mashed potatoes or steamed rice.

Nutritional Data:
Calories: 280 | Carbohydrates: 10g | Protein: 30g | Fat: 13g | Fiber: 1g

Rosemary Garlic Roast Beef

⭐⭐⭐⭐⭐ | Preparation Time: 15 mins | Cooking Time: 60 mins | Portion Size: 6

Ingredients:

1 kg beef roast

4 garlic cloves, minced

2 tbsp fresh rosemary, chopped

1 tbsp olive oil

Salt and pepper to taste

Instructions:

Preheat oven to 180°C (350°F).

Mix garlic, rosemary, olive oil, salt, and pepper in a bowl.

Rub the mixture all over the beef roast.

Place the roast in a baking dish and cook in the oven for about 60 minutes or until desired doneness.

Let it rest for 10 minutes before slicing.

Serve with roasted vegetables or a fresh salad.

Nutritional Data:
Calories: 320 | Carbohydrates: 2g | Protein: 50g | Fat: 12g | Fiber: 0.5g

Spicy Turkey Lettuce Wraps

⭐⭐⭐⭐⭐ | Preparation Time: 20 mins | Cooking Time: 15 mins | Portion Size: 4

Ingredients:

500g ground turkey

1 red bell pepper, finely chopped

2 green onions, sliced

2 tbsp low-sodium soy sauce

1 tbsp chili paste

1 tsp olive oil

8 lettuce leaves (Romaine or Iceberg)

Instructions:

Heat olive oil in a skillet over medium-high heat.

Add ground turkey and cook until browned, breaking it apart with a spatula.

Add bell pepper and cook for another 3-4 minutes.

Stir in soy sauce and chili paste and cook for an additional 2 minutes.

To serve, spoon the turkey mixture onto lettuce leaves and top with green onions.

Nutritional Data:
Calories: 240 | Carbohydrates: 8g | Protein: 30g | Fat: 10g | Fiber: 2g

Balsamic Glazed Chicken Thighs

⭐⭐⭐⭐⭐ | Preparation Time: 10 mins | Cooking Time: 40 mins | Portion Size: 4

Ingredients:

8 boneless, skinless chicken thighs

1/2 cup balsamic vinegar

2 tbsp honey

2 garlic cloves, minced

1 tbsp olive oil

Salt and pepper to taste

Instructions:

Preheat oven to 200°C (390°F).

In a bowl, mix balsamic vinegar, honey, garlic, salt, and pepper.

In a skillet, heat olive oil over medium-high heat. Brown the chicken thighs on both sides.

Pour the balsamic mixture over the chicken thighs.

Transfer the skillet to the oven and bake for 25-30 minutes or until chicken is cooked through.

Serve with steamed vegetables or a grain of choice.

Nutritional Data:
Calories: 290 | Carbohydrates: 12g | Protein: 28g | Fat: 14g | Fiber: 0g

Lean Beef and Broccoli Stir-Fry

☆ ☆ ☆ ☆ | Preparation Time: 20 mins | Cooking Time: 15 mins | Portion Size: 4

Ingredients:

500g lean beef strips

2 cups broccoli florets

1 red bell pepper, sliced

2 tbsp low-sodium soy sauce

1 tbsp ginger, minced

2 garlic cloves, minced

1 tbsp olive oil

1 tsp sesame oil

Instructions:

In a bowl, combine soy sauce, ginger, and garlic. Add beef strips, ensuring they are well coated, and marinate for 10 minutes.

Heat olive oil in a large skillet or wok over medium-high heat. Add beef strips and stir-fry until they are browned but not fully cooked. Remove from the skillet and set aside.

In the same skillet, add sesame oil, broccoli, and bell pepper. Stir-fry until the vegetables are slightly tender.

Return the beef to the skillet and cook for another 3-4 minutes or until everything is well combined and heated.

Serve with brown rice or whole grain noodles.

Nutritional Data:

Calories: 300 | Carbohydrates: 9g | Protein: 30g | Fat: 16g | Fiber: 2g

Paprika Chicken Skewers

☆ ☆ ☆ ☆ ☆ | Preparation Time: 25 mins (including marination) | Cooking Time: 12 mins | Portion Size: 4

Ingredients:

4 boneless, skinless chicken breasts, cut into chunks

2 tbsp paprika

1 tbsp garlic powder

2 tbsp lemon juice

1 tbsp olive oil

Salt to taste

Wooden skewers, soaked in water for 20 minutes

Instructions:

In a large bowl, combine paprika, garlic powder, lemon juice, olive oil, and salt. Add chicken chunks and marinate for at least 15 minutes.

Preheat a grill or grill pan over medium heat. Thread chicken chunks onto the soaked wooden skewers.

Grill for 5-6 minutes on each side or until chicken is thoroughly cooked.

Serve with a fresh salad or grilled vegetables.

Nutritional Data:

Calories: 220 | Carbohydrates: 3g | Protein: 25g | Fat: 11g | Fiber: 1g

Lemon Herb Roasted Pork Tenderloin

☆ ☆ ☆ ☆ ☆ | Preparation Time: 10 mins |Cooking Time: 25 mins | Portion Size: 4

Ingredients:

1 pork tenderloin (about 500g)

2 tbsp lemon juice

2 tbsp fresh rosemary, chopped

2 tbsp fresh thyme, chopped

2 garlic cloves, minced

1 tbsp olive oil

Salt and pepper to taste

Instructions:

Preheat oven to 200°C (390°F).

In a bowl, combine lemon juice, rosemary, thyme, garlic, olive oil, salt, and pepper.

Rub the herb mixture all over the pork tenderloin.

Place the tenderloin in a roasting pan and bake for 20-25 minutes or until it reaches the desired level of doneness.

Let it rest for 5 minutes before slicing.

Serve with roasted vegetables or a whole grain of choice.

Nutritional Data:

Calories: 280 | Carbohydrates: 3g | Protein: 30g | Fat: 15g | Fiber: 1g

Mediterranean Grilled Lamb Chops

★ ★ ★ ★ ★ | Preparation Time: 20 mins | Cooking Time: 14 mins | Portion Size: 4

Ingredients:

8 lamb chops

2 tbsp fresh oregano, chopped

1 tbsp fresh rosemary, chopped

2 garlic cloves, minced

Zest and juice of 1 lemon

2 tbsp olive oil

Salt and pepper to taste

Instructions:

In a bowl, mix together oregano, rosemary, garlic, lemon zest, lemon juice, olive oil, salt, and pepper.

Coat lamb chops with the marinade and let them marinate for at least 15 minutes.

Preheat grill to medium-high heat.

Grill lamb chops for about 6-7 minutes on each side or until desired doneness.

Serve with a side of Mediterranean salad or couscous.

Nutritional Data:

Calories: 310 | Carbohydrates: 3g | Protein: 34g | Fat: 18g | Fiber: 1g

Tandoori Spiced Turkey Breast

★ ★ ★ ★ ★ | Preparation Time: 20 mins (plus marination time) | Cooking Time: 35 mins | Portion Size: 4

Ingredients:

500g turkey breast

3 tbsp plain yogurt

1 tbsp lemon juice

1 tbsp paprika

1 tsp turmeric

1 tsp ground cumin

1 tsp ground coriander

1 tsp chili powder

2 garlic cloves, minced

Salt to taste

Instructions:

In a bowl, mix together yogurt, lemon juice, paprika, turmeric, cumin, coriander, chili powder, garlic, and salt.

Coat turkey breast with the marinade and let it marinate for at least 2 hours or overnight.

Preheat oven to 180°C (350°F).

Place the marinated turkey breast in a baking dish and bake for 30-35 minutes or until turkey is cooked through.

Slice and serve with a side of roasted vegetables.

Nutritional Data:

Calories: 250 | Carbohydrates: 5g | Protein: 40g | Fat: 8g | Fiber: 1g

Herbed Chicken Meatballs with Tomato Sauce

★ ★ ★ ★ ★ | Preparation Time: 20 mins | Cooking Time: 25 mins | Portion Size: 4

Ingredients:

500g ground chicken

2 tbsp fresh parsley, chopped

1 tbsp fresh basil, chopped

1 egg

1/4 cup breadcrumbs

1 can (400g) low-sodium diced tomatoes

2 garlic cloves, minced

1 tsp olive oil

Salt and pepper to taste

Instructions:

In a bowl, combine ground chicken, parsley, basil, egg, breadcrumbs, salt, and pepper. Mix until well combined.

Shape the mixture into meatballs.

In a skillet, heat olive oil over medium heat. Add garlic and sauté for 1 minute.

Add canned tomatoes and bring to a simmer.

Place the meatballs in the tomato sauce, cover, and simmer for 20-25 minutes or until meatballs are cooked through.

Serve with whole wheat spaghetti or zoodles.

Nutritional Data:

Calories: 290 | Carbohydrates: 15g | Protein: 28g | Fat: 13g | Fiber: 3g

Balsamic Glazed Beef Medallions

★ ★ ★ ★ ★ | Preparation Time: 15 mins | Cooking Time: 20 mins | Portion Size: 4

Ingredients:

4 beef medallions (approximately 150g each)

3 tbsp balsamic vinegar

1 tbsp honey

1 tbsp Dijon mustard

1 garlic clove, minced

1 tbsp olive oil

Salt and pepper to taste

Instructions:

In a bowl, whisk together balsamic vinegar, honey, Dijon mustard, garlic, salt, and pepper.

Coat beef medallions with half of the mixture and let marinate for at least 10 minutes.

Heat olive oil in a skillet over medium-high heat. Cook beef medallions to your preferred doneness, approximately 4-6 minutes per side for medium-rare.

Remove beef from skillet and set aside. Add the remaining balsamic mixture to the skillet and simmer until slightly thickened.

Drizzle sauce over beef medallions before serving.

Nutritional Data:

Calories: 295 | Carbohydrates: 8g | Protein: 28g | Fat: 16g | Fiber: 0g

Rosemary Garlic Roast Chicken

★ ★ ★ ★ ★ | Preparation Time: 20 mins | Cooking Time: 60 mins | Portion Size: 4

Ingredients:

1 whole chicken (about 1.5 kg)

2 tbsp fresh rosemary, finely chopped

3 garlic cloves, minced

1 lemon, zested and juiced

2 tbsp olive oil

Salt and pepper to taste

Instructions:

Preheat oven to 200°C (390°F).

In a bowl, mix together rosemary, garlic, lemon zest, lemon juice, olive oil, salt, and pepper.

Rub the mixture all over the chicken, ensuring it's well-coated both outside and under the skin.

Place the chicken in a roasting pan, breast side up. Roast in the oven for approximately 60 minutes or until the chicken is cooked through and the skin is golden brown.

Let it rest for 10 minutes before carving.

Serve with your choice of roasted or steamed vegetables.

Nutritional Data:

Calories: 410 | Carbohydrates: 4g | Protein: 35g | Fat: 28g | Fiber: 1g

Spiced Pork Loin with Apple Chutney

★★★★★ | Preparation Time: 20 mins | Cooking Time: 50 mins | Portion Size: 4

Ingredients:

500g pork loin

2 apples, diced

1 onion, finely chopped

2 tbsp apple cider vinegar

1 tbsp honey

1 tsp ground cinnamon

1/2 tsp ground nutmeg

1 tbsp olive oil

Salt and pepper to taste

Instructions:

Preheat oven to 190°C (375°F).

Rub pork loin with salt, pepper, and half of the ground cinnamon. Place in a roasting pan.

Roast pork loin in the oven for about 40-50 minutes or until it's cooked through.

While the pork is roasting, heat olive oil in a skillet over medium heat. Add onions and cook until translucent.

Add apples, apple cider vinegar, honey, remaining cinnamon, and nutmeg. Cook for 10-12 minutes, stirring occasionally until the apples are tender and the mixture thickens.

Slice pork loin and serve with apple chutney on the side.

Nutritional Data:

Calories: 320 | Carbohydrates: 20g | Protein: 30g | Fat: 14g | Fiber: 3g

Honey Mustard Glazed Chicken Thighs

★★★★★ | Preparation Time: 15 mins | Cooking Time: 35 mins | Portion Size: 4

Ingredients:

4 boneless, skinless chicken thighs

2 tbsp honey

2 tbsp Dijon mustard

1 tbsp apple cider vinegar

1 garlic clove, minced

1 tbsp olive oil

Salt and pepper to taste

Instructions:

In a bowl, combine honey, Dijon mustard, apple cider vinegar, garlic, salt, and pepper.

Coat chicken thighs with the honey mustard mixture and let marinate for at least 15 minutes.

Preheat oven to 200°C (390°F).

In an oven-safe skillet, heat olive oil over medium heat. Add chicken thighs and sear for 2-3 minutes on each side until golden brown.

Transfer skillet to the oven and bake for 25-30 minutes, or until chicken is cooked through.

Serve with steamed broccoli or green beans.

Nutritional Data:

Calories: 265 | Carbohydrates: 10g | Protein: 24g | Fat: 14g | Fiber: 0g

Moroccan Beef Stew

★★★★★ | Preparation Time: 20 mins | Cooking Time: 2 hrs | Portion Size: 4

Ingredients:

500g lean beef stew meat, cubed

1 onion, chopped

2 garlic cloves, minced

2 carrots, sliced

1 can (400g) low-sodium diced tomatoes

1 tsp ground cumin

1 tsp ground coriander

1/2 tsp cinnamon

1/4 tsp cayenne pepper

2 tbsp olive oil

500 ml beef broth (low-sodium)

Salt and pepper to taste

Instructions:

In a large pot, heat olive oil over medium heat. Add onions and garlic and sauté until translucent.

Add beef cubes and brown on all sides.

Stir in cumin, coriander, cinnamon, cayenne, salt, and pepper. Mix well.

Add diced tomatoes, carrots, and beef broth. Bring to a boil.

Reduce heat, cover, and let simmer for 1.5 to 2 hours until beef is tender and flavors meld together.

Adjust seasoning if needed and serve hot.

Nutritional Data:

Calories: 295 | Carbohydrates: 14g | Protein: 28g | Fat: 15g | Fiber: 4g

---

Grilled Pork Chops with Mango Salsa

✦ ✦ ✦ ✦ | Preparation Time: 20 mins | Cooking Time: 15 mins | Portion Size: 4

Ingredients:

4 boneless pork chops

1 ripe mango, diced

1/2 red bell pepper, diced

1/4 red onion, finely chopped

1 jalapeño, seeded and finely chopped (optional)

Juice of 1 lime

1 tbsp chopped fresh cilantro

1 tbsp olive oil

Salt and pepper to taste

Instructions:

Preheat grill to medium-high heat.

Rub pork chops with olive oil, salt, and pepper. Grill for about 6-7 minutes on each side, or until cooked to your preference.

While the pork chops are grilling, combine mango, red bell pepper, red onion, jalapeño, lime juice, cilantro, salt, and pepper in a bowl. Mix well to make the mango salsa.

Serve grilled pork chops with a generous spoonful of mango salsa on top.

Nutritional Data:

Calories: 280 | Carbohydrates: 20g | Protein: 25g | Fat: 12g | Fiber: 3g

Vegan

Quinoa & Black Bean Stuffed Peppers

⭐⭐⭐⭐ | Preparation Time: 20 mins | Cooking Time: 35 mins | Portion Size: 4

Ingredients:

4 bell peppers, any color

1 cup cooked quinoa

1 can (15 oz) black beans, drained and rinsed

1 cup corn kernels

1 tsp ground cumin

1 tsp paprika

Salt and pepper to taste

2 tbsp olive oil

Fresh cilantro for garnish

Instructions:

Preheat the oven to 190°C (375°F).

Cut off the tops of the bell peppers and remove the seeds.

In a mixing bowl, combine quinoa, black beans, corn, cumin, paprika, salt, and pepper.

Stuff each bell pepper with the quinoa mixture and place in a baking dish.

Drizzle with olive oil.

Cover with aluminum foil and bake for 35 minutes or until the peppers are tender.

Garnish with fresh cilantro before serving.

Nutritional Data:

Calories: 230 | Carbohydrates: 40g | Protein: 8g | Fat: 5g | Fiber: 9g

Hearty Lentil & Vegetable Soup

⭐⭐⭐⭐⭐ | Preparation Time: 15 mins | Cooking Time: 45 mins | Portion Size: 6

Ingredients:

1 cup green lentils, rinsed

2 carrots, diced

2 celery stalks, diced

1 onion, diced

2 garlic cloves, minced

1 can (15 oz) diced tomatoes

6 cups vegetable broth

1 tsp dried thyme

2 bay leaves

Salt and pepper to taste

2 tbsp olive oil

Instructions:

In a large pot, heat olive oil over medium heat. Sauté onions, carrots, and celery until softened.

Add garlic and sauté for another 2 minutes.

Stir in lentils, diced tomatoes, vegetable broth, thyme, bay leaves, salt, and pepper.

Bring to a boil, then reduce heat and let simmer for 35-40 minutes or until lentils are tender.

Remove bay leaves before serving.

Nutritional Data:

Calories: 210 | Carbohydrates: 35g | Protein: 12g | Fat: 4g | Fiber: 15g

Creamy Avocado & Spinach Pasta

⭐⭐⭐⭐ | Preparation Time: 10 mins | Cooking Time: 15 mins | Portion Size: 4

Ingredients:

300g whole wheat spaghetti

2 ripe avocados

2 cups fresh spinach

2 garlic cloves

Juice of 1 lemon

Salt and pepper to taste

2 tbsp olive oil

Cherry tomatoes for garnish

Instructions:

Cook spaghetti according to package instructions.

In a food processor, blend avocados, spinach, garlic, lemon juice, salt, and pepper until smooth.

Drain pasta and return to the pot. Mix in the creamy avocado sauce and stir until well combined.

Serve topped with cherry tomatoes.

Nutritional Data:

Calories: 420 | Carbohydrates: 60g | Protein: 12g | Fat: 18g | Fiber: 10g

Spiced Chickpea & Kale Salad with Lemon Tahini Dressing

✿ ✿ ✿ ✿ ✿ | Preparation Time: 20 mins | Cooking Time: 0 mins | Portion Size: 4

Ingredients:

1 can (15 oz) chickpeas, drained and rinsed

4 cups kale, finely chopped

1 cucumber, diced

1 red bell pepper, diced

1 tsp ground cumin

1 tsp paprika

Dressing:

1/4 cup tahini

Juice of 1 lemon

1 garlic clove, minced

2 tbsp water

Salt to taste

Instructions:

In a large mixing bowl, combine chickpeas, kale, cucumber, bell pepper, cumin, and paprika.

For the dressing, whisk together tahini, lemon juice, garlic, water, and salt until smooth.

Pour the dressing over the salad and toss well to coat.

Serve immediately.

Nutritional Data:

Calories: 250 | Carbohydrates: 35g | Protein: 10g | Fat: 10g | Fiber: 8g

Oven-Roasted Root Vegetable Medley

✿ ✿ ✿ ✿ ✿ | Preparation Time: 15 mins | Cooking Time: 40 mins | Portion Size: 4

Ingredients:

2 carrots, peeled and sliced

2 parsnips, peeled and sliced

1 sweet potato, peeled and diced

2 beets, peeled and diced

3 tbsp olive oil

1 tsp dried rosemary

Salt and pepper to taste

Instructions:

Preheat oven to 200°C (400°F).

In a large bowl, toss the vegetables with olive oil, rosemary, salt, and pepper.

Spread on a baking sheet in a single layer.

Roast for 35-40 minutes, or until vegetables are tender and slightly caramelized, stirring halfway through.

Serve warm.

Nutritional Data:

Calories: 200 | Carbohydrates: 30g | Protein: 3g | Fat: 8g | Fiber: 6g

Stir-fried Tofu with Gingered Vegetables

✿ ✿ ✿ ✿ ✿ | Preparation Time: 20 mins | Cooking Time: 15 mins | Portion Size: 4

Ingredients:

200g firm tofu, cubed

2 tbsp soy sauce

1 tbsp grated ginger

2 garlic cloves, minced

1 bell pepper, sliced

1 zucchini, sliced

2 tbsp sesame oil

2 green onions, chopped

1 tbsp sesame seeds

Instructions:

In a bowl, marinate tofu cubes with soy sauce, ginger, and garlic. Set aside for 15 minutes.

Heat sesame oil in a skillet or wok over medium-high heat.

Add the marinated tofu and stir-fry until golden.

Add bell pepper and zucchini, stir-frying until vegetables are tender-crisp.

Garnish with green onions and sesame seeds before serving.

Nutritional Data:

Calories: 160 | Carbohydrates: 10g | Protein: 8g | Fat: 10g | Fiber: 2g

---

Sweet Potato & Black Bean Tacos

⭐ ⭐ ⭐ ⭐ ⭐ | Preparation Time: 20 mins | Cooking Time: 30 mins | Portion Size: 4

Ingredients:

2 large sweet potatoes, peeled and diced

1 can (15 oz) black beans, drained and rinsed

1 tsp ground cumin

1 tsp smoked paprika

2 tbsp olive oil

8 small corn tortillas

1 avocado, sliced

Fresh cilantro, chopped

Lime wedges for serving

Instructions:

Preheat oven to 200°C (400°F).

Toss sweet potatoes with olive oil, cumin, and paprika on a baking sheet.

Roast for 25-30 minutes until tender and lightly browned, stirring halfway through.

Warm tortillas according to package instructions.

Assemble tacos with roasted sweet potatoes, black beans, avocado slices, and fresh cilantro.

Serve with lime wedges on the side.

Nutritional Data:

Calories: 340 | Carbohydrates: 55g | Protein: 10g | Fat: 10g | Fiber: 13g

---

Vegan Lentil Loaf

⭐ ⭐ ⭐ ⭐ ⭐ | Preparation Time: 20 mins | Cooking Time: 45 mins | Portion Size: 6

Ingredients:

2 cups cooked green lentils

1 onion, finely chopped

2 garlic cloves, minced

1 carrot, grated

1/2 cup rolled oats

1/2 cup breadcrumbs

2 tbsp flaxseed meal mixed with 6 tbsp water (flax egg)

2 tbsp tomato paste

1 tsp dried basil

1 tsp dried oregano

Salt and pepper to taste

2 tbsp olive oil

Instructions:

Preheat oven to 190°C (375°F).

In a skillet, sauté onions and garlic in olive oil until translucent.

In a food processor, pulse lentils, sautéed onion mixture, carrot, oats, breadcrumbs, flax egg, tomato paste, basil, oregano, salt, and pepper until combined.

Press mixture into a loaf pan.

Bake for 45 minutes until the top is browned and firm to the touch.

Let cool for a few minutes before slicing and serving.

Nutritional Data:
Calories: 250 | Carbohydrates: 40g | Protein: 13g | Fat: 5g | Fiber: 10g

---

Zucchini Noodle Pesto Bowl

☆ ☆ ☆ ☆ | Preparation Time: 20 mins | Cooking Time: 5 mins | Portion Size: 4

Ingredients:
4 zucchinis, spiralized into noodles
1 cup cherry tomatoes, halved
1/4 cup pine nuts, toasted

Pesto:
2 cups fresh basil leaves
1/4 cup olive oil
2 garlic cloves
1/4 cup nutritional yeast
Salt and pepper to taste

Instructions:
For the pesto, blend basil, olive oil, garlic, nutritional yeast, salt, and pepper in a food processor until smooth.

In a large bowl, toss zucchini noodles with the pesto until well coated.

Top with cherry tomatoes and toasted pine nuts before serving.

Nutritional Data:
Calories: 220 | Carbohydrates: 15g | Protein: 7g | Fat: 17g | Fiber: 5g

---

Desserts

Almond Joy Chia Pudding

⭐ ⭐ ⭐ ⭐ | Preparation Time: 10 mins | Cooking Time: 0 mins (Chill for 3 hours) | Portion Size: 4

Ingredients:

3 cups almond milk

1/2 cup chia seeds

2 tbsp unsweetened cocoa powder

2 tbsp honey or maple syrup

1 tsp vanilla extract

1/4 cup shredded coconut

1/4 cup sliced almonds

Instructions:

Mix almond milk, chia seeds, cocoa powder, honey, and vanilla extract in a bowl.

Chill the mixture in the fridge for at least 3 hours, or overnight.

Serve topped with shredded coconut and sliced almonds.

Nutritional Data:

Calories: 210 | Carbohydrates: 24g | Protein: 6g | Fat: 11g | Fiber: 9g

Berry Bliss Oat Bars

⭐ ⭐ ⭐ ⭐ ⭐ | Preparation Time: 15 mins | Cooking Time: 30 mins | Portion Size: 8

Ingredients:

2 cups rolled oats

1 cup mixed berries (frozen or fresh)

1/4 cup honey or maple syrup

1/2 cup unsweetened applesauce

1 tsp vanilla extract

Instructions:

Preheat the oven to 175°C (350°F) and line an 8x8 baking dish with parchment paper.

Mix all ingredients in a bowl until well combined.

Press the mixture firmly into the baking dish.

Bake for 30 minutes, or until the edges start to turn golden brown.

Let cool before cutting into bars.

Nutritional Data:

Calories: 140 | Carbohydrates: 30g | Protein: 3g | Fat: 1.5g | Fiber: 4g

Chocolate Avocado Mousse

⭐ ⭐ ⭐ ⭐ ⭐ | Preparation Time: 10 mins | Cooking Time: 0 mins | Portion Size: 4

Ingredients:

2 ripe avocados

1/4 cup unsweetened cocoa powder

1/4 cup almond milk

1/4 cup honey or maple syrup

1 tsp vanilla extract

Instructions:

Blend all ingredients in a food processor until smooth.

Chill in the fridge for at least 1 hour before serving.

Nutritional Data:

Calories: 230 | Carbohydrates: 27g | Protein: 3g | Fat: 15g | Fiber: 8g

Date & Walnut Energy Bites

⭐ ⭐ ⭐ ⭐ ⭐ | Preparation Time: 20 mins | Cooking Time: 0 mins | Portion Size: 12

Ingredients:

1 cup pitted dates

1 cup walnuts

2 tbsp cocoa powder

1 tsp vanilla extract

A pinch of salt

Instructions:

Blend all ingredients in a food processor until a dough-like consistency forms.

Roll into 1-inch balls and place on a parchment paper-lined tray.

Chill in the fridge for at least 1 hour before serving.

Nutritional Data:

Calories: 90 | Carbohydrates: 12g | Protein: 2g | Fat: 5g | Fiber: 2g

Flaxseed & Blueberry Muffins

⭐ ⭐ ⭐ ⭐ | Preparation Time: 15 mins | Cooking Time: 20 mins | Portion Size: 12

Ingredients:

1 1/2 cups whole wheat flour

1/2 cup ground flaxseed

1/2 cup honey or maple syrup

1 tsp baking powder

1/2 tsp baking soda

1 cup fresh or frozen blueberries

1/2 cup unsweetened almond milk

2 large eggs

1/4 cup coconut oil, melted

Instructions:

Preheat the oven to 175°C (350°F) and line a muffin tin with paper liners.

In a mixing bowl, combine flour, flaxseed, baking powder, and baking soda.

In another bowl, whisk together honey, almond milk, eggs, and coconut oil.

Add the wet ingredients to the dry ingredients and mix until just combined. Fold in the blueberries.

Pour the batter into muffin cups and bake for 20 minutes, or until a toothpick comes out clean.

Nutritional Data:

Calories: 170 | Carbohydrates: 26g | Protein: 4g | Fat: 7g | Fiber: 4g

Gluten-Free Banana Pancakes

⭐ ⭐ ⭐ ⭐ ⭐ | Preparation Time: 10 mins | Cooking Time: 15 mins | Portion Size: 6

Ingredients:

2 ripe bananas, mashed

1/2 cup almond flour

2 large eggs

1 tsp baking powder

1/2 tsp vanilla extract

A pinch of salt

Instructions:

Mix all ingredients in a bowl until well combined.

Heat a non-stick skillet over medium heat. Pour 1/4 cup portions of batter onto the skillet.

Cook for 2-3 minutes on each side, or until golden brown.

Serve with fresh fruit and a drizzle of honey.

Nutritional Data:

Calories: 110 | Carbohydrates: 12g | Protein: 4g | Fat: 6g | Fiber: 2g

Honey-Sweetened Lemon Sorbet

⭐ ⭐ ⭐ ⭐ | Preparation Time: 10 mins | Cooking Time: 0 mins (Freeze for 4 hours) | Portion Size: 6

Ingredients:

Zest and juice of 3 lemons

1/2 cup honey

2 cups water

Instructions:

In a bowl, mix together the lemon zest, juice, honey, and water until well combined.

Pour the mixture into an ice cream maker and churn according to the manufacturer's instructions.

Transfer to a freezer-safe container and freeze for at least 4 hours before serving.

Nutritional Data:
Calories: 90 | Carbohydrates: 25g | Protein: 0g | Fat: 0g | Fiber: 0g

Dark Chocolate & Almond Bark

★ ★ ★ ★ ★ | Preparation Time: 10 mins | Cooking Time: 0 mins (Chill for 2 hours) | Portion Size: 8

Ingredients:
200g dark chocolate (at least 70% cocoa)
1/2 cup roasted almonds, roughly chopped
1/4 cup dried cranberries

Instructions:
Melt the dark chocolate in a microwave or using a double boiler method.

Once melted, fold in the chopped almonds and cranberries.

Spread the mixture on a parchment paper-lined tray, ensuring it's about 1/2-inch thick.

Chill in the fridge for at least 2 hours.

Once set, break into pieces and serve.

Nutritional Data:
Calories: 160 | Carbohydrates: 12g | Protein: 3g | Fat: 12g | Fiber: 3g

Chia Seed & Berry Pudding

★ ★ ★ ★ | Preparation Time: 15 mins | Cooking Time: 0 mins (Chill for 4 hours) | Portion Size: 4

Ingredients:
1/4 cup chia seeds
1 cup almond milk (unsweetened)
1 tbsp honey
1 tsp vanilla extract

1/2 cup mixed berries (like blueberries, strawberries, and raspberries)

Instructions:
Mix chia seeds, almond milk, honey, and vanilla in a bowl.

Let it sit for about 10 minutes and then mix again to avoid clumps.

Cover and chill in the fridge for at least 4 hours, preferably overnight.

Before serving, top with mixed berries.

Nutritional Data:
Calories: 100 | Carbohydrates: 12g | Protein: 3g | Fat: 5g | Fiber: 5g

Pistachio & Rose Water Mousse

★ ★ ★ ★ ★ | Preparation Time: 15 mins | Cooking Time: 0 mins | Portion Size: 4

Ingredients:
1/2 cup shelled pistachios, plus extra for garnish
1 cup heavy cream
2 tbsp honey
1 tsp rose water

Instructions:
Blend the pistachios in a food processor until they form a fine powder.

In a separate bowl, whip the heavy cream until stiff peaks form.

Gently fold in the pistachio powder, honey, and rose water.

Divide the mixture into serving glasses and chill for at least 2 hours.

Garnish with chopped pistachios before serving.

Nutritional Data:
Calories: 220 | Carbohydrates: 10g | Protein: 3g | Fat: 20g | Fiber: 1g

Coconut & Mango Lassi

⭐⭐⭐⭐⭐ | Preparation Time: 10 mins | Cooking Time: 0 mins | Portion Size: 4

Ingredients:

1 ripe mango, peeled and chopped

1 cup coconut yogurt

1/2 cup coconut milk

1 tbsp honey

A pinch of cardamom powder

Instructions:

Blend all ingredients together in a blender until smooth.

Pour into glasses and chill for about 30 minutes.

Serve cold.

Nutritional Data:

Calories: 130 | Carbohydrates: 18g | Protein: 2g | Fat: 6g | Fiber: 2g

Pumpkin Spiced Muffins

⭐⭐⭐⭐⭐ | Preparation Time: 15 mins | Cooking Time: 20 mins | Portion Size: 12

Ingredients:

1 1/2 cups whole wheat flour

1 cup pumpkin puree

1/2 cup honey or maple syrup

1/4 cup olive oil or melted coconut oil

2 tsp baking powder

1 tsp cinnamon

1/2 tsp nutmeg

1/4 tsp cloves

1/4 tsp salt

Instructions:

Preheat the oven to 180°C (350°F) and line a muffin tin with paper liners.

In a large mixing bowl, combine all the ingredients and mix until well combined.

Divide the batter evenly among the muffin cups.

Bake for 20-25 minutes or until a toothpick inserted into the center of a muffin comes out clean.

Allow to cool before serving.

Nutritional Data:

Calories: 150 | Carbohydrates: 25g | Protein: 3g | Fat: 5g | Fiber: 3g

Yogurt Granola with Strawberry, Blueberry, and Cashew

⭐⭐⭐⭐⭐ | Preparation Time: 10 minutes | Cooking Time: 0 minutes | Portion Size: 2 servings

Ingredients:

- 1 cup coconut yogurt
- 1/2 cup granola (preferably low sugar or homemade)
- 1/4 cup fresh strawberries, sliced
- 1/4 cup fresh blueberries
- 2 tbsp cashews, roughly chopped

Instructions:

1. Start by preparing the fruits. Wash the strawberries and blueberries under cold water, then gently pat them dry using a kitchen towel.
2. Slice the strawberries into thin slices, ensuring that they are uniformly cut for a better presentation.
3. In a mixing bowl, add the coconut yogurt and give it a quick stir to ensure a smooth consistency.
4. Take two serving bowls and start layering your parfait. Begin with a layer of coconut yogurt at the bottom of each bowl.
5. Next, add a layer of granola over the yogurt, evenly dividing between the two bowls.
6. Layer the sliced strawberries and blueberries on top of the granola.

7. Sprinkle the roughly chopped cashews over the fruits.
8. For a final touch, add a dollop or drizzle of coconut yogurt on top. This step is optional but makes for a delightful presentation.
9. Serve immediately, or you can refrigerate them for up to an hour before serving if you prefer a chilled parfait.

Nutritional Data:
Calories: 280 | Carbs: 30g | Protein: 7g | Fats: 15g | Sugars: 10g | Fiber: 4g

Date & Walnut Bliss Balls

⭐⭐⭐⭐⭐ | Preparation Time: 15 mins | Cooking Time: 0 mins | Portion Size: 15
Ingredients:
1 cup dates, pitted
1 cup walnuts
1 tbsp chia seeds
1 tbsp flaxseed meal
1 tsp vanilla extract
A pinch of salt

Instructions:
In a food processor, blend dates and walnuts until they form a sticky mixture.

Add chia seeds, flaxseed meal, vanilla extract, and salt. Blend until well combined.

Roll the mixture into small balls and place on a tray lined with parchment paper.

Chill in the refrigerator for at least 1 hour before serving.

Nutritional Data:
Calories: 100 | Carbohydrates: 12g | Protein: 2g | Fat: 6g | Fiber: 2g

Strawberry & Chia Jam

⭐⭐⭐⭐ | Preparation Time: 10 mins | Cooking Time: 15 mins | Portion Size: 10
Ingredients:
2 cups strawberries, hulled and chopped
2 tbsp chia seeds
2 tbsp honey or maple syrup
1 tsp lemon juice

Instructions:
In a saucepan, cook strawberries over medium heat until they soften and release their juices.

Mash the strawberries with a fork or a potato masher.

Add chia seeds, honey, and lemon juice. Stir well.

Simmer for 10-15 minutes until the jam thickens.

Remove from heat and let it cool. Transfer to a jar and refrigerate.

Nutritional Data:
Calories: 40 | Carbohydrates: 8g | Protein: 1g | Fat: 1g | Fiber: 2g

Oat and Berry Crumble

⭐⭐⭐⭐⭐ | Preparation Time: 15 mins | Cooking Time: 25 mins | Portion Size: 6
Ingredients:
2 cups mixed berries (fresh or frozen)
1 cup rolled oats
1/2 cup chopped nuts (almonds, walnuts, or pecans)
1/4 cup maple syrup or honey
1/4 cup coconut oil, melted
1 tsp cinnamon
A pinch of salt

Instructions:
Preheat the oven to 180°C (350°F).

Spread berries at the bottom of a baking dish.

In a bowl, mix oats, nuts, maple syrup, coconut oil, cinnamon, and salt.

Sprinkle the oat mixture over the berries.

Bake for 25 minutes or until the top is golden.

Serve warm.

Nutritional Data:

Calories: 220 | Carbohydrates: 30g | Protein: 5g | Fat: 10g | Fiber: 4g

Almond Joy Energy Bites

★ ★ ★ ★ | Preparation Time: 20 mins | Cooking Time: 0 mins | Portion Size: 15

Ingredients:

1 cup almonds

1/2 cup unsweetened shredded coconut

1/4 cup cocoa powder

8 medjool dates, pitted

1 tbsp coconut oil

1 tsp vanilla extract

Instructions:

In a food processor, blend almonds, coconut, cocoa powder, dates, coconut oil, and vanilla extract.

Once the mixture becomes sticky, form into small balls.

Place them on a lined tray and refrigerate for at least 1 hour before serving.

Nutritional Data:

Calories: 110 | Carbohydrates: 12g | Protein: 3g | Fat: 7g | Fiber: 3g

Heart-Healthy Banana Ice Cream

★ ★ ★ ★ ★ | Preparation Time: 10 mins | Cooking Time: 0 mins | Portion Size: 4

Ingredients:

4 ripe bananas, sliced and frozen

1/4 cup almond milk

1 tsp vanilla extract

Optional toppings: berries, chopped nuts, or dark chocolate chips

Instructions:

Blend frozen banana slices, almond milk, and vanilla extract in a high-speed blender or food processor until smooth.

You should achieve a creamy ice cream texture.

Serve immediately with your favorite toppings or store in the freezer for later.

Nutritional Data:

Calories: 110 | Carbohydrates: 28g | Protein: 1g | Fat: 1g | Fiber: 3g

Cinnamon Apple Chips

★ ★ ★ ★ | Preparation Time: 10 mins | Cooking Time: 2 hours | Portion Size: 4

Ingredients:

2 large apples, thinly sliced

1 tsp cinnamon

1 tbsp maple syrup (optional)

Instructions:

Preheat your oven to 100°C (210°F).

Arrange apple slices on a baking sheet lined with parchment paper.

Sprinkle with cinnamon and drizzle with maple syrup if desired.

Bake for 2 hours or until the apple slices are dried and edges curl up. Halfway through, turn the slices over.

Let them cool and store in an airtight container.

Nutritional Data:

Calories: 60 | Carbohydrates: 16g | Protein: 0g | Fat: 0g | Fiber: 3g

Fresh Fruit and Berry Salad

☆ ☆ ☆ ☆ ☆ | Preparation Time: 15 minutes | Cooking Time: 0 minutes | Portion Size: 4 servings

Ingredients:

- 1 cup strawberries, halved
- 1 cup fresh blueberries
- 1 cup raspberries
- 1 cup mango, diced
- 1 cup kiwi, sliced
- 1/2 cup pecan or almonds (optional)
- Juice of 1 lemon
- 1 tablespoon honey (optional)
- Fresh mint leaves for garnish

Instructions:

1. In a large bowl, combine the strawberries, blueberries, raspberries, mango, and kiwi. Gently mix to combine.
2. In a separate small bowl, mix the lemon juice and honey until the honey is fully dissolved. This will create a light dressing for the salad.
3. Pour the lemon and honey dressing over the fruit in the large bowl and gently mix to coat the fruit evenly.
4. If desired, add pecan or almonds for some crunch.
5. Transfer the fruit salad to individual plates or a large serving bowl.
6. Garnish with fresh mint leaves before serving.

Nutritional Information: Calories: 150 kcal | Carbohydrates: 35g | Protein: 3g | Fat: 2g (if nuts added) | Fiber: 7g | Sugars: 25g | Cholesterol: 0mg | Sodium: 5mg

30-Day Meal Plan

Day	Breakfast	Lunch	Dinner	Total Calories
1	WHOLESOME OAT AND BERRY PARFAIT	QUINOA TABBOULEH WITH FRESH HERBS	LEMON-DILL BAKED SALMON	1600
2	SPINACH AND MUSHROOM EGG WHITE OMELETTE	MEDITERRANEAN CHICKPEA SALAD WITH LEMON VINAIGRETTE	HERB-CRUSTED GRILLED CHICKEN SALAD	1700
3	QUINOA AND FRUIT BREAKFAST SALAD	HEARTY LENTIL AND VEGETABLE STEW	QUICK SEAFOOD PAELLA WITH SAFFRON	1500
4	HEART-LOVING ALMOND BUTTER TOAST WITH SLICED STRAWBERRIES	BARLEY RISOTTO WITH MUSHROOMS AND SPINACH	ROSEMARY GARLIC PORK TENDERLOIN	1650
5	MANGO AND CHIA SEED SMOOTHIE BOWL	CHICKPEA AND SPINACH CURRY	CREAMY AVOCADO & SPINACH PASTA	1550
6	SWEET POTATO AND BLACK BEAN BREAKFAST BURRITO	BLACK BEAN AND QUINOA STUFFED PEPPERS	ZESTY LIME SHRIMP SKEWERS	1600
7	GOLDEN TURMERIC AND GINGER PORRIDGE	CREAMY BUTTERNUT SQUASH AND LENTIL SOUP	LEMON-THYME TURKEY SKEWERS	1550
8	HEART-HEALTHY BLUEBERRY PANCAKES (WITH ALMOND FLOUR)	MILLET AND VEGGIE STIR-FRY WITH TAMARI GLAZE	BALSAMIC GLAZED TURKEY MEATBALLS	1700
9	ZESTY LEMON AND POPPY SEED OVERNIGHT OATS	RED LENTIL DAHL WITH SPINACH	GARLIC LEMON BUTTER SHRIMP	1650

10	NUTTY BANANA AND FLAXSEED MUFFINS	BUCKWHEAT GROATS WITH SAUTÉED VEGGIES	HONEY-MUSTARD GRILLED CHICKEN BREASTS	1600
11	TANGY GREEK YOGURT WITH MIXED BERRIES AND HONEY DRIZZLE	BARLEY AND LENTIL SOUP WITH KALE	ZESTY LIME AND GARLIC SHRIMP TACOS	1100
12	NUTTY BANANA AND FLAXSEED MUFFINS	MEDITERRANEAN CHICKPEA SALAD WITH LEMON VINAIGRETTE	SPICED PORK LOIN WITH APPLE CHUTNEY	1150
13	CINNAMON WALNUT QUINOA BREAKFAST PUDDING	BULGUR WHEAT AND VEGGIE STIR-FRY	LEMON-THYME TURKEY SKEWERS	1075
14	REFRESHING BERRY AND KIWI SMOOTHIE BOWL	MUNG BEAN AND RICE PILAF	ZESTY LEMON SALMON	1120
15	HEARTY OATS AND APPLE PORRIDGE	SORGHUM SALAD WITH MIXED VEGGIES	HONEY MUSTARD GLAZED CHICKEN THIGHS	1090
16	ZESTY LEMON AND POPPY SEED PANCAKES	BEEF AND BROCCOLI STIR-FRY	QUINOA & BLACK BEAN STUFFED PEPPERS	1130
17	MANGO AND ALMOND BUTTER SMOOTHIE	BALSAMIC GLAZED BEEF MEDALLIONS	OVEN-ROASTED ROOT VEGETABLE MEDLEY	1160
18	GOLDEN TURMERIC AND GINGER PORRIDGE	LENTIL STUFFED BELL PEPPERS	GINGER SOY SALMON BOWL	1080
19	FIBER-RICH MUESLI WITH NUTS AND SEEDS	CHILI LEMON CRAB CAKES	SPICED CHICKPEA & KALE SALAD WITH LEMON TAHINI DRESSING	1140
20	HEARTFELT GREEN SMOOTHIE	SPELT PASTA WITH LENTIL BOLOGNESE	BALSAMIC GLAZED CHICKEN THIGHS	1050

21	HEART-HEALTHY BLUEBERRY PANCAKES (WITH ALMOND FLOUR)	ROSEMARY GARLIC ROAST CHICKEN	VEGAN LENTIL LOAF	1150
22	SWEET POTATO AND BLACK BEAN BREAKFAST BURRITO	CHILI LIME COD FILLETS	PAPRIKA PORK TENDERLOIN	1130
23	CHIA SEED AND COCONUT OVERNIGHT PUDDING	LEMON HERB PRAWNS AND ZOODLES	MEDITERRANEAN STUFFED CHICKEN BREASTS	1100
24	MANGO SALSA MAHI-MAHI	BARLEY RISOTTO WITH MUSHROOMS AND SPINACH	SPICED LAMB CHOPS WITH MINT YOGURT	1180
25	WHOLESOME SPINACH AND FETA EGG MUFFINS	BLACK BEAN AND QUINOA STUFFED PEPPERS	LEMON-DILL BAKED SALMON	1125
26	TANGY GREEK YOGURT WITH MIXED BERRIES AND HONEY DRIZZLE	MILLET AND VEGGIE STIR-FRY WITH TAMARI GLAZE	HERB-STUFFED ROAST CHICKEN	1140
27	ZESTY LEMON AND POPPY SEED OVERNIGHT OATS	HERBED TUNA STEAKS WITH OLIVE RELISH	ZUCCHINI NOODLE PESTO BOWL	1085
28	SWEET POTATO AND BLACK BEAN BREAKFAST BURRITO	SPICED CHICKPEA AND FARRO BOWL	ROSEMARY GARLIC PORK TENDERLOIN	1150
29	HEARTFELT WHOLE GRAIN TOAST WITH AVOCADO AND TOMATO	RED LENTIL DAHL WITH SPINACH	HERB-CRUSTED LAMB CHOPS	1130
30	FIBER-RICH MUESLI WITH NUTS AND SEEDS	FARRO AND ROASTED BEET SALAD	LEMON HERB ROASTED PORK TENDERLOIN	1100

Measurement Conversion Chart

Volume Equivalents (Liquid)

US Standard	US Standard (ounces)	Metric (approximate)
2 tablespoons	1 fl. oz.	30 mL
¼ cup	2 fl. oz.	60 mL
½ cup	4 fl. oz.	120 mL
1 cup	8 fl. oz.	240 mL
1½ cups	12 fl. oz.	355 mL
2 cups or 1 pint	16 fl. oz.	475 mL
4 cups or 1 quart	32 fl. oz.	1 L
1 gallon	128 fl. oz.	4 L

Volume Equivalents (Dry)

US Standard	Metric (approximate)
⅛ teaspoon	0.5 mL
¼ teaspoon	1 mL
½ teaspoon	2 mL
¾ teaspoon	4 mL
1 teaspoon	5 mL
1 tablespoon	15 mL
¼ cup	59 mL
⅓ cup	79 mL
½ cup	118 mL
⅔ cup	156 mL
¾ cup	177 mL
1 cup	235 mL
2 cups or 1 pint	475 mL
3 cups	700 mL
4 cups or 1 quart	1 L

Oven Temperatures

Fahrenheit (F)	Celsius (C) (approximate)
250°F	120°C
300°F	150°C
325°F	165°C
350°F	180°C
375°F	190°C
400°F	200°C
425°F	220°C
450°F	230°C

Weight Equivalents

US Standard	Metric (approximate)
1 tablespoon	15 g
½ ounce	15 g
1 ounce	30 g
2 ounces	60 g
4 ounces	115 g
8 ounces	225 g
12 ounces	340 g
16 ounces or 1 pound	455 g

Recipe Index

Made in the USA
Las Vegas, NV
13 December 2023

82669427R00052